Back to Tonic

by Eugene Kiepura

First published by Faith Books & MORE

ISBN 978-1-939761-18-7

Printed in the United States of America
This book is printed on acid-free paper.

 3255 Lawrenceville-Suwanee Rd. | Suite P250
Suwanee, GA 30024
publishing@faithbooksandmore.com
faithbooksandmore.com

Ordering Information:
Quantity sales. Special discounts are available on quantity purchases by corporations, associations, and others. For details, contact the publisher at the address above.

Orders by U.S. trade bookstores and wholesalers. Please contact Ingram Book Company: Tel: (800) 937-8000; Email: orders@ingrambook.com or visit ipage.ingrambook.com.

Disclaimer
The purpose of this book is to empower, educate, and offer hope. The authors of the book achieved that through their own experiences, expertise, and research. Consequently, this book should only be used as a road map. This book is not intended to be nor is it represented as legal advice. The authors are not liable or responsible, to any person, or entity, for any and all claims, demands, damages, causes of action, suits in equity of whatever kind or nature, caused or alleged to have been caused, directly or indirectly, by the information contained in this book or the authors' past or future negligence or wrongful acts.

For Jan, Janene, and Cherie

In memory of Jacob

Acknowledgements

Above all, I thank my family. This book would not have been possible without their standing behind me, not in just the writing process but throughout the experiences described in this book. I am especially grateful to my wife, best friend and sounding board Jan; my writing coach and believer Cherie Garza; and my inspiration and advocate Janene Preston.

I am grateful to the following people who read all or part of the manuscript and provided valuable feedback: Annette Clarke, Carl Koerner, Stewart Scott, Joanne Zapchenk, Arleen Duffy, Alice Kiepura, Randy Roberts, Bob Kiepura, Joyce Kiepura, Debra Miller and Megan Bates.

I am appreciative of the encouragement of Charlene Ann Baumbich and Susan Wakefield Dal Porto.

I am grateful for the opportunity to work with Nicole Antoinette Smith (Faith Books & MORE). I especially want to thank my editor Gloria Spencer, and my cover designer Neon Alfred (www.neonalfred.com).

Finally, I am forever indebted to my mother and father, Mary and Edward Kiepura; for their unshakable example of faithfulness.

Contents

Preface

"The most horrible crisis imaginable would be to discover that God is a stranger, and it is too late to do anything about it."

There have been many books written by authors who express the confidence they have in the God of the Bible. What happens to those of us who have lost that confidence? We're not bad people. Trusting God just isn't as simple as some make it out to be; especially when He appeared to have sat silently on the sidelines while our world was crumbling apart. I suppose some people can accept tragedy as being "God's will" and then stick their heads in the sand to avoid facing the challenging questions that fill the empty space left in tragedy's wake. I tried ... It didn't work. Trust has no value in our hour of crisis if it amounts to nothing more than words.

Losing a child has best been described as "Waiting to exhale." Try it; take a deep breath and hold it... keep holding it. Can you feel the tension and the increasing discomfort? Imagine waking each morning to that same anxiety, wondering if you'll ever be able to release it. Your irreplaceable treasure has been lost forever; there's no coming back.

I had been told that about 78% of marriages in which a child dies end in divorce. Maybe that's because each parent looked at it as "My tragedy." Jan and I saw it as "Our tragedy." She and I have always been of one accord. We shared this, or most of it. I'm a protector. I'm supposed to be strong. I made the mistake of shielding her from what was inwardly killing me because I refused to show weakness.

I'm sure that just fueled the depression that began to take hold of me. Depression is a clammy, stiff feeling where nothing seems worth doing. My mind was ensnared in a wasteland, void of value and energy. I wanted to think about Jake, but when I did it only reminded me that he was dead. Was that all I could ever expect? Would I always view his life through the window of his death?

PROLOGUE

"Tonic"

"We must be willing to let go of the life we planned so as to have the life that is waiting for us."

~ Joseph Campbell

I entered the 1980s a content man with a wife I adored and children I cherished; all was right with God. The peace of Christianity had blossomed in my life and flooded me with the unwavering confidence that all was well and would remain that way.

Having discovered what it meant to be "Born Again" five years prior, I reached new levels in my faith. I loved the pastor at the small church we attended in East Hazel Crest, Illinois, and I was even getting used to the people.

My wife Jan and I attended Sunday school classes and taught children in the junior church on a rotating basis. We seldom missed a Sunday service; in fact I would go on my own when she was unable to go. I developed a thirst for God unlike anything I had ever known before.

As our family grew, we moved to a church closer to our home with a larger youth group so our children could get involved in the youth activities. I became a deacon at the new church and began to lead small group studies. Becoming fairly well-versed in the New Testament, I enjoyed debating others who were not.

Everything made sense to me then. I read through the Bible with a yellow highlighter pen in my hand and marked the verses that jumped out at me. Each time I reread a book, I would highlight any new insights with a different color pen.

Once when I opened my Bible in class, a guy next to me said, "It looks like a rainbow landed in there."

Prayer was easy for me, just like talking to my earthly father. Once I started talking it was hard to stop. Sometimes I felt as if I was hoarding God's attention all to myself, but I didn't care; God was mine.

God was accessible and life made perfect sense. All was good... until it all fell apart...

PART I

"Dominant"

Chapter 1

Irreplaceable Treasure

"One day, a son asked his father,
'Why is it always the best people who die?'
The father answered, 'Son, if you are in a meadow,
which flowers do you pick? The worst ones or the best?'"
                                        ~ Author Unknown

I never saw it coming. I never imagined it would turn out the way it did. There should have been a joyous return. There should have been a celebration... There wasn't. I wasn't prepared for it... Who would be?

Two decades later, I found myself sitting on a rooftop in Titanyen, Haiti, watching a thunderstorm passing over the central mountain range. It was a familiar storm, much like the one that had escorted me and the remains of my son Jacob home from Mexico twenty years earlier. Only this time instead of accompanying me the storm was bidding me farewell. As it rolled off into the distance it reminded me of how my earlier perception of God had also rolled out of my life.

I had expected a much different God. He was supposed to be my guardian, not the seemingly callous being who allowed me so much pain. I couldn't wrap my mind around the concept of a God who permitted tragedy to strike the lives of those He supposedly loved. The easiest way to have dealt with my disappointment would have been to just stop believing in Him, but that wasn't possible; He was very real to me. I couldn't deny that all of creation could have only come from one Supreme Being. Within me resided the knowledge of the existence of a deity I could no longer grasp, the puzzle I couldn't solve. That weighed heavily on my conscience as I tried to move on. It got to the point where I had to either resolve the resentment harbored within me or accept the unattractive notion of living out the remainder of my life in the constant grasp of depression.

I wanted my life back... I wanted my God back... I wanted my son back... the son I was so proud to father.

Jake

Jacob was born on Friday, May 26, 1978; the same day the Chicago Cubs defeated the St. Louis Cardinals six to nothing, in St Louis. It just doesn't get much better than that! If that wasn't a sign of great things to come, I didn't know what was. I was beaming! I wanted a son in the worst way. I couldn't wait to start teaching him how to throw a ball, catch a fish and build a campfire. Satisfying my need to celebrate this joyous occasion, I did something I'd always wanted to do. I bought a half gallon of chocolate ice cream and ate the entire thing. After numerous brain freezes and a long night of suffering through ice cream hangover, I vowed to never do that again!

Our first child, Janene, had kept us up at night with colic. We were so pleased that Jake didn't suffer from the same condition. That pleasure vanished the evening we discovered he had a different nightly problem. It was 1:45am. Jan woke me asking, "What's that noise?" As I cleared the sleep from my eyes and listened, I heard a squeaking, springy kind of sound. I got up and crept through the house toward the thin stream of light visible under Jacob's bedroom door. The noise was definitely coming from inside his room. I pushed the door open and there he was, riding his rocking horse.

Jacob was a year and a half old and he didn't understand why someone would need to sleep when there were things to do. He had climbed out of his crib onto the dresser and turned on the light. Then he slipped down to the floor and up onto his rocking horse. This became one of his nightly habits that kept Jan and me busy the first few years. He tested us whenever he could; not a bad kid, he was just defining his margins.

Once Jan sat at the kitchen table with him for an hour and a half trying to get him to pick up the placemat he'd purposely thrown on the floor. At one point she physically took his hands and made him pick it up and place it on the table. He proceeded to throw it right back on the floor. Finally she said, "Look Jake; neither one of us is leaving this table until you pick up the placemat." He stared at her as if to test her sincerity, then climbed down and picked it up. He was quite the time investment, but he was well worth it.

Jacob was a curious boy, an adventurer who saw life as his playing field. We had to fence in the backyard because he didn't understand boundaries. If he saw something that interested him—and everything did—he just went for it. Everything was fascinating to him.

One snowy winter day I came home to find Jake's small boot prints in the snow leading to a large, dark hole in the ground.

Chapter 1: Irreplaceable Treasure

The old septic tank in the backyard had caved in. Here, in front of me, was a two-foot-diameter hole, and a few feet below the surface, still, black water.

Have you ever experienced one of those moments when you think you have lost or broken an irreplaceable treasure, an unrecoverable accident that strips you of all hope for tomorrow?

The air was cold and void of sound. The planet seemed to pause for a moment, leaving me with this Twilight Zone feeling of being the only person left alive on Earth. My heart fell through my shoes as I looked down at that cold, black water. It felt as if I were standing on the very edge of a cliff, and I began to lose my balance. A shudder of terror passed through my body. I ran to the house and, as calmly as possible, asked Jan, "Where's Jake?"

She said he had gone to Jason's house. Jason was his best friend and lived directly behind us.

I insisted she call to check if he were still there.

"What's wrong?" she said.

I barked back, "Please, just do it!"

Uneasily, she dialed the number. Sure enough, Jake was there.

"What the heck is going on?" she snapped. I brought her to the window and pointed to the cave-in. We both stood there silently and stared out the window, imagining what could have happened. Jan fell to her knees, sobbing, thanking God Jake was all right. How could parents possibly survive the loss of a child, their irreplaceable treasure?

We loved our children and heavily invested our time into their lives. It wasn't something we decided we should do as good parents; we just wanted to. That time with them was not only important to us, it was one of our greatest joys in life. Jan painstakingly sewed Halloween costumes for each of them every year, and they would be so excited to get dressed up and show them off at school. We had treasure hunts in our backyard and made life-sized board games in our driveway using the kids as the playing pieces. As often as we could afford it, we would take them to a cabin on Boot Lake near Mercer, Wisconsin, where we enjoyed just being together.

Shirley, the resort owner, liked Jacob. Many kids would come in and out of her lodge, taking a break from the beach to have a snack or play games. Most kids barely noticed the sweet old lady standing behind the counter. Jacob wasn't most kids. He had a knack for not just noticing people, but for making them feel as if they mattered. As a result, he mattered to them as well. She told us he would say hi and wave to her every time he walked by, no matter how many times that was. One summer during our stay she took his picture and hung the photo on the wall in her lodge bar room. It remained there for years.

One night an angry storm rolled over the lake; the kind of storm that demonstrates nature's tremendous power. I loved storms and decided to head outside for a look. As usual, Jake followed close behind. The intensity of the wind blew the porch door out of my hand and our belongings started flying throughout the cabin. Suddenly, there was a loud smack followed by a deafening scream. It was coming from our youngest, Cherie. A bat had been caught by the storm and thrown against the window pane. It frantically struggled to free itself from the force of the wind that pinned it against the glass.

Jake and I abandoned our curiosity watching God's power played out in nature and scrambled to find shelter. We pushed the dinner table against the stone fireplace and huddled with the family underneath. We knew when it was time to catch a thrill and when it was time to hug the gals we loved. We all held each other a little closer that night. At the time it was a frightening experience, but now we cherish looking back on those moments of bonding as a family.

Jan started working evenings at H&R Block. I looked after the kids while she was at work. In all, we had three. Jake was sandwiched between two sisters, Janene and Cherie. As soon as Jan would pull out the driveway at night the TV channel changed to WWF Wrestling, pillows came off the beds, and mayhem broke out. That was our secret. Jan would have had a fit if she had known. She hated violence and didn't want the kids exposed to it. But the kids and I knew better; this stuff was fun. After an evening of pile drivers and throwing each other around the living room, I'd put the kids to bed and clean up the mess.

Jan was none the wiser until the night she returned home early and caught us in full combat mode watching the movie, Rambo. She was fuming. Everyone—including me—was sent to their rooms. Jan meant well, and eventually she came to accept the fact that I was just another one of the kids.

I didn't want to be the kind of dad that just worked and supported his family. I wanted to be a friend, a playmate. I'm not talking about the guy who buys booze for his kids to look cool; I'm talking about being an invested teacher and friend. I wanted them to grow up knowing me as a trusted companion. There's more to being a father than structure and authority. My dad had always taken time for me. He loved our family and his example of fatherhood was etched into my mind. Jan and I took time for our children.

I played like a kid. While Jan was out in the evenings preparing other people's taxes the kids and I could be found taking the blankets off the beds and building connecting tents throughout the house, building snow forts, or playing hide and seek.

Chapter 1: Irreplaceable Treasure

I was delighted when Jacob reached the age to be able to join me in some of the things I liked to do. My dad lived through the Great Depression and learned how to provide for his family. Like some kind of MacGyver, he was a genius when it came to improvising repairs by utilizing his stash of old bolts and iron straps. Dad grew vegetables that my mom canned and he regularly devised various contraptions and procedures that simplified most household tasks. That's what he taught me. He wasn't much of a sportsman. I wish he could have added fishing and hunting to the things he did. I learned those skills on my own. When Jake reached the age of six I started taking him with me.

We'd fish for blue gills out of my canoe at Willow Slough Wildlife Area in Indiana. The gills there where huge, sometimes nine or ten inches; no lie. We'd stay out until it began to get dark and then head home with our catch. As Jake got more familiar with fishing equipment I taught him to catch bass with plastic worms. Many grown men cannot do that, but Jake could. What a joy it was to watch my son recognize the tap of a bass picking up the worm, set the hook and bring it in.

We kept the blue gills but released the bass. Grasping the fish by its lower jaw, Jake would lower it into the water and hold it until it seemed ready to swim away under its own power then he'd let it go. I'm not sure what he liked more, catching or releasing them.

Back to Tonic

As Jake got a little older I took him to the Kankakee River where I taught him to wade for small-mouth bass. It's a good thing Jan never witnessed this because she would have put a stop to it quicker than you can say, "What the heck is the matter with you?" But guys know that nothing is really fun unless there's at least a little risk involved.

Once while fishing the river we stumbled across this little haven near an island along hunting area seven. It seemed untouched by human hands and we declared it our secret place. We spent many days there fishing for bass and exploring the exposed roots of great trees washed clean of soil from years of river current flowing through them. We often sat in the shade of those old trees, Jake listening to stories of my youth. He'd ask details about outhouses and chicken coops, oil stoves and well water. I'd tell him about how milk was delivered to houses in glass bottles and how if you set an empty bottle on the counter by a window the sunlight would cause the cardboard cap to pop off. He wanted to hear stories about my chores as a kid, my favorite being burning the trash. There was an art to creating the perfect fire that would completely dispose of the contents of our fifty-five gallon garbage barrel. Jake was good at making campfires, and he could relate to my love of the dancing flames.

We started hunting together when he was around ten years old. Squirrel hunting is a good way to teach a boy to sit quietly in the woods. At first he sat right by me. Watching his every move, I'd talk him through the shot as a squirrel came within range. He was doing fine, and one day he asked if he could go over the ridge and sit by himself. It was hard to grant that request, but I let him go, watching tensely as he disappeared over the ridge. After about 20 minutes, a shot rang out. I jumped to my feet, but didn't know what to do. Do I run over there to see if he is alright? Do I stay here and wait for him to call? Deciding to creep up to the ridge and see what was going on, I spotted him with a squirrel in his hand. He sat down against a tree and gazed at the squirrel for a while. He then started scanning the trees for another one. I remember thinking, "Well, I guess he's a hunter now." Slipping back down the ridge, I waited for him to come to me.

He became really good at shooting squirrels. Jan and the girls wouldn't eat squirrel, and he and I could only eat so much, so we decided to get creative. My mom had a chicken cacciatore recipe that called for red wine, peas, mushrooms, onions, tomatoes and spices. We decided to substitute squirrel meat for the chicken. It smelled great and when the girls came home, we told them we had made chicken cacciatore for dinner. We explained that we had used dark meat instead of the usual breast meat the recipe called for. Jake nervously prepared their plates, and to our delight, they dove right in. "This is good Dad," they said. My eyes met Jake's, and we just shared a small smile. We never said a word about what they were eating. Years later, I finally confessed. They didn't take it very well.

Back to Tonic

Girls are great, and I treasure mine, but a dad needs a son. A dad doesn't necessarily know what to do with daughters. Tea parties are fun, and building doll houses is even better, but I'm not a girl. I'm only guessing at what makes them happy. Boy stuff is more a dad's element. Jake wasn't just my son; he was my buddy, my cohort.

Chapter 2

The Unimaginable

"That's the worst pain I've ever felt... I went straight to the ground after that one... I had to take a knee. I was just trying not to throw up."[2]

(MLB player Adam LaRoche on being hit by a fastball)

It was about 8:00pm on the 30th day of June, 1992. I stood outside the DuWayne Motel in West Chicago with my roommate. We were attending welding certification classes at the C&NW Railroad training center nearby. We both enjoyed hunting and fishing. As we stood there looking out on the woods that surrounded us, we each told stories about past seasons. Many of my stories included my favorite partner, my fourteen-year-old son Jacob. As we talked, we watched a raccoon working his way up a tree line until he was within several feet of us. A huge owl landed silently nearby. The woods began uttering their nightly clamor. The evening air felt cool. All seemed well.

July 1st, 6:00am, I awoke suddenly. I felt as if I had been thrust into a sitting position. A strange sensation quivered through my body. Looking out the window, I scanned the woods. Nothing seemed unusual. I climbed out of bed and prepared for school.

The hot day was made even more unbearable by the protective leather welding gear we had to wear. Everyone was glad to see class end for the day. We returned to the motel. I sat with three of the guys under a huge shade tree and had a beer. We talked about our families, crime, and religion. I couldn't help thinking about Jacob; he would be home from Mexico in three days.

On Sunday, June 14, Jacob had left on a three-week missionary trip to Mexico. He was accompanied by Juan,

Chapter 2: The Unimaginable

the youth pastor of our church, his son Jacob, and two other boys, Stephen and Brian. I was so proud of my son. I couldn't wait to see him and hear about his experiences. As the other guys continued talking, I slipped back against the tree and stared into the blue sky. My thoughts now were only of Jake.

I decided to go take a shower and get some dinner. As I opened the door to my room, the phone was ringing. I picked it up. There was no one on the line. It rang again with the same result. That happened three or four more times. I remember thinking it might be Jan, but she was supposed to call later that night. The phone rang again. Finally, I heard Jan's voice.

"Honey, come home. I need you."

"What's wrong?"

"I'd rather not tell you over the phone. Just come home. I need you. Now."

Her voice was filled with tense emotion, struggling to speak as if under the strain of a great weight.

"I'm on my way," I promised. We'd been together long enough for me to know not to press her further at that moment. She was devastated and whatever had happened would affect our lives like nothing we had ever experienced before. I packed my bags and left immediately.

I turned off the radio in the truck because I was afraid to listen to it. I prayed that whatever had happened, God would help us through it. I kept repeating Proverbs 3:5-6:

> *"Trust in the Lord with all your heart and lean not on your own understanding. In all your ways acknowledge Him and He will make your paths straight."*

I must have repeated it twenty times.

It was rush hour in Chicago compounded by construction; traffic was very heavy. It took over two hours to get home. That provided me a lot of time to think and pray. I started to break down what information I had. Thoughts bounded around in my head like a pinball.

I knew whatever had happened didn't require me to rush because she didn't tell me to hurry. Therefore, no one was dying; but someone could have died.

It must be a death; if it were anything else, she would have told me.

Why wouldn't she tell me who it was?

It had to be my mom, dad, or one of the kids. She would have told me if it had been anyone else.

Chapter 2: The Unimaginable

I prayed some more.

My mind was racing. My first thought was Jacob. He was far from home and something could have gone terribly wrong. Could it have been Janene? It was about the time she would have been driving to work; could she have had an accident? I then thought of Cherie; she could have been hit by a car while riding her bike. I prayed, *"God, don't let it be one of my children."* Then I thought of my mom and dad. Something could have happened to them.

I didn't know what to think, but my gut feeling was that something terrible had happened to one of those five people I cherished most. I prayed for the strength to be able to handle whatever had happened. I repeated the verses from Proverbs again and again. I didn't want to lose any of them.

As I got closer to home I began to tremble uncontrollably. I couldn't stand not knowing, but I didn't want to find out. I turned onto our street and saw a lot of cars at our house. Ours was in the driveway, so I knew Janene hadn't been in an accident. Most of the cars belonged to friends from church. I thought, *"Oh God; it's Jake! Why Jake?"*

I pulled into the driveway, but didn't want to get out of the truck. Jan was waiting at the door. I hurried toward her saying, *"It's Jake, isn't it?"*

She nodded. Then she and the girls grabbed me, wailing the most dreadful howl I had ever heard. Unable to cry, I just held them and helplessly glanced at the people sitting around our living room. There was nothing I could do or say to comfort the three people I loved more than anything. Holding them was all I knew to do.

"What happened?"

Jan told me there had been an auto accident.

"What about the others?"

"They're all gone."

All gone! How could that be? Those words still ring in my ears. It just didn't seem right. I wanted to scream, *"God, what are you doing?"* Instead, a feeling of numbness overcame me. Any ability to reason abandoned me.

The information we had was very sketchy. At some point we heard there was one survivor. Could it be Jake? Jan and I prayed they had mixed up the identities and mistakenly reported him as one of the deceased. Our prayers depicted a roller coaster of emotions. One minute we begged God to name Jake as the only survivor, the next we pleaded for forgiveness for our selfishness amid our friends who faced the same terrible position.

People from the church were making arrangements to get us to the airport. We had to pack. What did one need to pack to retrieve the body of his son? I stared at the suitcase and didn't know what to put in it. Several times I tried waking myself from what seemed to be a bad dream.

The phone rang; it was Mom. She sounded so heartbroken. I was worried about her and Dad, so I tried to be strong for them. What I really wanted was to crawl into their laps and have them cradle me like a child.

Our friends left after a while. Jan and I just paced back and forth, not knowing what to do. We needed to get ourselves ready to retrieve Jake's body, but couldn't concentrate for more than a couple minutes at a time. My brother John stopped by and gave us some extra money in case we ran into unanticipated expenses on the journey. I grabbed him, and I finally began to sob. He was at a loss for words. He told me if I had any trouble in Mexico I should contact the American Embassy because they were there to help.

My sister Arleen offered to stay with our girls. They were so distraught we found it very hard to leave them behind. A friend from church pulled up to the house and loaded our luggage into his van. It was time to leave for the airport. We started off on the longest trip of our lives.

The ride to the airport seemed to take forever. We were joined by Juan's wife Pat, Juan's brother, Brian's parents Harilyn and Ken, and Oscar, pastor of a Spanish church in Chicago Heights. Our flight didn't leave until 4:00am. We sat waiting, just staring into the distance. I still couldn't believe what was happening. There was no conversation; I just waited, like a man on Death Row moving second-by-second closer to a dreadful reality.

The flight took us to Monterey, Mexico, where we had to get off the plane and go through customs. After re-boarding, we took off over the Sierra Madre Occidental Mountains and landed in San Luis Potosi.

The airport was very small. When the plane landed we exited down a staircase on the tarmac and walked to the terminal. I didn't speak Spanish. An airport employee seemed to be motioning for me to stand in some designated area. Not knowing what to do, I nervously changed positions until he seemed satisfied. It was all very confusing.

Finally our bags showed up and we were allowed to exit the room. We met Pastor Hector from the church in San Luis Potosi where the boys had spent some of their time. His son, Hector Jr., along with his friend Samuel, had also been in the crash. Hector Jr. was the sole survivor.

Pastor Hector was accompanied by his friend Ruben, and the two of them loaded our bags into their cars. Juan's parents and brother along with Oscar left the airport in Hector's car.

Chapter 2: The Unimaginable

We followed behind in Ruben's car, but were separated from the others when the road became blocked by a shepherd herding his goats. What kind of airport shares its property with a herd of goats?

Ruben didn't speak a word of English. We had to rely on Pat—who had a limited grasp of the language—to interpret for us. It was very hard to understand where we were going or what we were doing. We finally figured out that we were going to the town of San Luis De La Pas several hours away.

Observing the scenery as we traveled, I found it both beautiful and filthy, a totally different form of existence than I was used to. There were vast areas of desert-like sandy terrain containing large stands of cacti. The locals inhabited small huts nestled within the cactus stands. This scene was back-dropped by mountains in every direction. It was so strange to see donkeys pulling wagons and people riding bikes right alongside us as we traveled down busy Highway 57. The beauty of the countryside was spoiled by a never-ending deposit of litter and inhabitants who appeared destitute.

We learned the accident had occurred early the previous morning on that very highway. A semi-truck passing another at a speed of nearly 100 miles per hour had struck the boys' van head-on, dragging it under the truck's cab for nearly three-quarters of a mile. On impact, Hector was ejected out the sliding side door, leaving him with many injuries, but alive.

Traveling that same strip of highway, we observed trucks relentlessly passing vehicles with little regard for on-coming traffic. Having learned how the boys had died, watching the huge trucks approaching at such high speeds caused us to feel very apprehensive. Ken was feeling so nervous I told Pat to ask Ruben to slow down and, if possible, avoid passing other vehicles. After that Ruben drove so slowly I felt like getting out and running.

We came to a place where men were pulling the cab and trailer of a truck out of the ditch. I turned back and could clearly see from the cab's damage that it had been in a head-on collision. I kept that to myself as I didn't want to upset the others. Later I learned that was the site of the accident and was the very truck that had killed our boys.

The entire time we traveled I kept trying to believe there had been some mistake and Jake was alive. I thought maybe they had assumed he was dead and when I got there I would show them he was breathing. I clung to the hope that somehow he would be alive.

We pulled into San Luis De La Pas early in the afternoon on July 2nd. By now I had been without sleep for over thirty hours. The antique-looking town consisted of old structures and narrow cobblestone roads. The buildings were set right out at the road's edge and jammed together as if they were one continuous building. The residents looked just like their town: withered and neglected by time. For some reason, the town had no running water that day.

We went directly to some sort of morgue to identify the boys, but were advised that the bodies were not yet ready to be viewed. We went to the Policía Federal headquarters. The office had large, open-air window openings. The locals were hanging in through the openings to see what was going on inside. We remained there for what seemed like hours attempting to answer questions and complete reports. Juan's brother and Pat did what translating they could for us.

I had no idea what was going on, and was angered by the apparent lack of compassion by some of the officials there. They seemed to be people of little importance acting important. One man holstering what appeared to be a Colt Single Action Army revolver on his right hip kept strutting back and forth in front of me. I didn't like the way he looked at me. It felt like he was trying to intimidate me. I didn't need more trouble; I just wanted to go to my son.

Eventually we were escorted back to what they referred to as a hospital where again we waited for quite a while. The place looked more like a maintenance facility than a hospital. Unlike the gleaming appearance of hospitals back home, this place was dingy. The floors were wet as if they had attempted to clean them with spray from a garden hose.

Oscar, from the Spanish church in Chicago Heights, was waiting there for us. He went to find out what was taking so long and was informed that the bodies were now ready to be viewed. They first took Oscar in alone. Returning to our group, he recommended that only one of us do the identification. I overheard him quietly tell Ken he didn't think he should go in. Ken asked if Brian was in one piece.

I volunteered to go. I needed to see Jake. I needed to know he was really dead. Again I felt like that man on Death Row inching closer and closer to an unavoidable finale. Walking through several passageways, we came to a cinderblock building. Oscar put his arm around me. He kept saying, *"Be strong, brother. Be strong."* A boy at the door gave me a cloth to hold over my mouth and nose.

I entered what was essentially a poorly-lit, empty room. It wasn't what I had expected. Three bodies lay on the dirty floor covered with a single bloody sheet. Two more sheets covered bodies lying on tables. The odor was overpowering, but it was not that of decaying corpses. It was more a mix of chemical and animal carcass odors.

Someone pulled the sheet off the bodies on the floor. There is a point where a damaged human body no longer looks human. Facial features contort hideously out of place and the look of terror becomes a permanently-fixed expression. I'd seen that kind of thing in horror films, but I never expected to see it in real life. I was shocked. I didn't recognize the first body. I silently prayed it wasn't Jake. After taking a closer look, I realized the other two bodies on the floor were Juan's son Jacob, and Steve.

My legs weakened. My lungs seemed to shudder as I tried to draw breath. With quivering lips I attempted to form words that I just could not utter. The awful moment had arrived and the tragedy became reality.

Pulling back the sheet from the body on the table revealed Jake. My heart broke. I felt as if a part of me flew screaming out the window. His body was torn and traumatized, covered with cuts and bruises. His wounds were closed in much the same way a football skin is laced together. He was covered with blood, both dry and damp. It was a dreadful sight. Taking a deep breath I forced out the words, *"That's my son."*

What does one do when looking upon his dead son? I wanted to touch him, but my gut feeling was not to because I may not want to be haunted by the memory of what he felt like. His injuries were so horrific I didn't know where to look. My eyes traveled around his body at high speed. Even with all the damage, he looked at rest, almost peaceful. I wished Jan were with me. I needed to be held by her. But I didn't want her to witness what I was seeing. This seemed so wrong, so unjust.

Next they uncovered Juan, the last body on the table. He had suffered a battering head injury. I could only be certain who he and the first body on the floor were through the process of elimination. After the identification I was led out of the room and back to the others. With eyes focused and full of dread, they watched as I approached. I looked at them, shook my head and said, *"It's them. You don't want to see."*

With more paperwork to take care of, we returned to the police station. They required us to identify the bodies by phone to some federal authority. The authorities would only release a body to a family member. Being that our pastor and his wife weren't with us, I pretended to be our pastor on the phone. I wasn't going to leave Mexico without their son.

While the others continued filling out paperwork at the police station, I was taken to see Juan's van. The boys had been writing journals while on the trip and we hoped to find them. I was looking for any information, photos or keepsakes that might provide us with an account of what they had been doing. It took some time to gain access to the van. It had been towed to a junkyard and the presence of an official was required before they would let me enter. This official claimed to be first on the scene of the accident. He affirmed that all but one had been dead when he arrived and he also determined that the truck driver's actions had caused the accident.

This official had a police report from Acapulco dated June 30th. It stated that while the boys were swimming in the ocean someone had broken into their van and stolen many of their possessions. He said that even more of their belongings had been looted at the accident site.

Chapter 2: The Unimaginable

When I finally got to see the van, I couldn't believe it. It was utterly crushed. I don't know how anyone could have lived through that accident. Hector survived only because he was sitting on the spare tire that had been temporarily stored inside the van after changing a flat. Upon impact, the side door had flown open, ejecting both the tire and Hector.

I pulled out what bags I could. Searching through them, I failed to find any journals. I continued pulling what I could out of the wreckage. Six men perching on a pile of scrap iron nearby watched me like buzzards waiting for their turn at a carcass. Much of the cargo was pinned under seats and between jagged pieces of metal. I needed to find those journals. They would describe the boys' last days, thoughts, and maybe even offer some surprises. I climbed into the wreckage. The sweltering heat made it feel like an oven. The interior appeared to have been sprayed with blood. Flies swarmed around the blood-soaked hair and pieces of flesh stuck to the roof. The rolling of my stomach had just about convinced me to exit the wreck when I spotted Jan's Bible wedged under what was left of the back seat. It was her Mother's Day gift from the kids and Jake had borrowed it for the trip. I pried out the crushed and blood-stained book. Jan still treasures it today.

And then, as if divinely placed on what remained of the dashboard, I saw a page torn from one of the hymnals the boys had used. The song was *The Haven of Rest*.

Back to Tonic

Continuing my search, I found Juan's wallet, some film, and eventually a few of the journals. Much of what remained were shattered pieces of Nintendo games, CDs, and other personal items. Sick to my stomach, I searched on until the official motioned that it was time to leave. I climbed out of the wreckage. There was no water pressure or means of cleaning my arms and hands now marked with blood from my search. Feeling defiled, I gathered the recovered items and headed back to the police headquarters.

On the way back, Hector told me Steve's and Juan's bodies needed to be cremated. They felt it would be best if the other bodies were cremated as well. I relayed that information to the other parents. We didn't like the idea of cremation, but agreed. I arranged for Jan to see Jake one last time before he was sent to the crematorium.

As pastel orange and violet hues of light from the setting sun painted the sky over the mountains, Jan said goodbye to Jake for the final time in his coffin, in an alley, on the back of a pickup truck.

We had a long drive back to San Luis Potosi to take Pat to the airport. She needed to get home since her girls had been at summer camp and were due to return the next day. They did not know about the accident and Pat wanted to be there for them when they found out. We decided Harilyn should accompany Pat.

We then learned there might not be enough seats for everyone on the next night's flight. Jan and I decided she should leave with Pat as well. Jan didn't want to leave me and I would have preferred to have her at my side, but we thought it best for her to go to our girls. That was a decision I would later regret.

Then Ken surprised me by announcing he also wanted to leave. I have to admit to feeling a tremendous load placed on my back. But believing most everything was under control, I told him to go with them.

I held Jan tightly and kissed her good-bye before they boarded the airplane for home. With their plane safely in the air, I went back to San Luis Potosi with Ruben, who didn't speak a word of English.

Chapter 3

Trial by Ordeal

"If you're going through hell, keep going."[4]
~ *Winston Churchill*

Mexico is not all rural poverty. There are modern urban areas, but most of my time was spent in locations that seemed to have been built in an era when automobiles were not factored into the plans. With narrow streets and little parking available, many people actually parked their cars inside their houses. I visited the home of an insurance representative whose car was parked directly behind his living room couch.

Ruben owned his own business and his home was in a more modern middle-class part of town. He and his wife had four children. The oldest girl spoke a few words in English, but not enough for us to really communicate. Ruben brought out an electronic translator. We attempted to use it, though it was a slow process and seldom relayed what we meant to say. Giving up on the translator, Ruben sent one of his sons down the street to get a boy named Ramón. Ramón had spent a year in the States where he had learned some English. With Ramón at hand, communication became much easier.

We ate dinner and went over the plans for the next day. I learned that after a morning funeral we would be sending the bodies to be cremated. Ruben asked if I needed anything. I told him I would like to get some rest as I had been awake for over forty hours. He showed me where I was to sleep and made arrangements for Ramón to spend the night so I could communicate with them when needed.

I spent another sleepless night. How I wished to have Jan

next to me. I had never known loneliness like that before. Thoughts of Jake ran through my mind like Morse code rattling in on a telegraph machine. Recollections of unfulfilled promises I'd made to Jake haunted me. I kept thinking about the treehouse he wanted that we had never gotten around to building. I cried out to God asking, *"How am I going to live without him?"* I prayed for strength. I asked for help to collect the boys' remains and return to my family as soon as possible. I looked to God for a revelation, but when I closed my eyes all I could see was Jake's dead body.

Early the next morning we went to a funeral home in San Luis Potosi. The place was filled with people who knew very little English. I saw the five caskets on display. At each one I opened the little door that covered their heads. They looked better since they had been cleaned up and dressed in clean clothes.

I stood over Jake for a long time. I could see traces of blood from his chest wounds staining the white shirt. I just stared at him and wondered if he had seen the terror of the accident. Was he awake? Did he witness the truck coming at them? Did he hear the squealing tires? Did he scream? I kept rubbing my fingers on the glass that covered his face. I wanted him back.

With no one to talk with and not really knowing what to do, I decided to walk around and thank people for coming. They started a funeral service and sang some songs, all in Spanish. When the service ended I walked outside. There was some kind of argument going on. I listened and quickly picked up that Juan's parents didn't want to send the bodies back to Chicago. I grabbed Juan's brother and asked him what was going on. He said Juan's parents wanted to bury Juan and his son Jacob in Salamanca, Mexico. I stepped in and told them I couldn't let them do that. Pat wanted the bodies back home. Juan's parents also had a problem with having the bodies cremated.

We argued for a while. Then from out of the blue a man came to inform me we needed to send the bodies to another town for cremation. It would be a four-hour trip and I would need to pay them an additional four thousand dollars.

What was this all about? Why did we pay to send the bodies to San Luis Potosi if they couldn't be cremated there? Were they just looking to get more money out of me? Was this a trick so Juan and Jacob could be buried in Mexico without me knowing about it? Could there possibly be any more pressure piled on me?

Angrily, I demanded to speak to the people in the office. Instead, Oscar escorted me away. I insisted on speaking to someone from the American Embassy.

The embassy had been contacted for help the day before while we were in San Luis De La Pas. That only resulted in a long wait on a lonely dirt road for the hope of help that had no intention of responding. Oscar talked to the funeral director who agreed to call the embassy for me. Again, I waited for hours, and again, no one showed up.

I decided to take the bodies as they were, fly to Texas and have them cremated there. They said paperwork to transport the bodies by airplane would take several weeks. I was feeling trapped. Every town seemed to have a different set of rules. I was beginning to think I might never get out of Mexico.

Determined to do whatever it took to get the boys home as soon as possible, I went along with sending the bodies elsewhere for cremation. Unexpectedly, the funeral director dropped the price of the cremation and promised to have the cremains back early the next day.

I don't know what it costs us to maintain our embassy in Mexico, but it is a waste of money. I found the embassy to be not only useless, but fraudulent as well. They made no attempt to contact the families with the news of the accident, nor did they meet us when we arrived. My requests for assistance were ignored. What they did do was arrive at the scene of the accident on the morning of July 1, acknowledge that U.S. Citizens had been killed and then simply instruct the Mexican officials to cremate the bodies. With that, they left. Done! In the midst of such a tragic experience I expected some personal assistance. Later I would find the embassy to be my greatest obstacle. I spent the day filling out more and more paperwork and kissing every butt I could in an effort to get the boys out of there.

The cremains were returned at about 1:30am. Ramón was too young to tag along with us at that time of night. Without him the language barrier made communication almost impossible. I just wanted to get home, so I didn't question the middle-of-the-night delivery. I paid the director and asked for a receipt. He made some indication as if he would give me one the next day.

By that point I didn't know who to trust. Everybody seemed to have their hands out. Every town we traveled through wanted me to pay a fee or have another funeral service. I was tired, aggravated and had had enough. I demanded a receipt right then and there, fearing that in the morning they would bill me again. Standing in front of him with my hand held out, I waited until he complied.

Completely unaware of what was going on, I later discovered that a small group of people were clandestinely working behind the scenes to help me bring the boys home. Given the language barrier, it was probably easier for them not to explain what they were doing. Most of our communication was done by means of pointing and hand motions. I was better off not knowing I was about to smuggle their cremains out of Mexico.

Chapter 3: Trial by Ordeal

Returning to Ruben's house about 2:30am, we found his wife up waiting for us. The dinner table was beautifully set and she had prepared a homemade chicken tortilla soup. She was so gracious and a source of comfort at a point in time when I most needed it. After dinner I went to bed for another sleepless night. I sought God's comfort in prayer, but instead wrestled with the feeling of being on my own.

The next day we went to the church in San Luis Potosi for another funeral service. Hector took me for a walk around the block. He showed me the library where our boys had spent some time. Strolling down a tree-lined walkway, I reached out and touched the low hanging leaves. I could picture the boys touching those branches in the same way. Like the scent of cologne lingering shortly after the wearer had left the room, I could almost feel their presence around me.

People began to pile into the church. The pews filled quickly. The service was all in Spanish, *"the language of heaven,"* they claimed. Numerous people stood and spoke. Many people cried.

I was motioned to come up to the front where I was handed a microphone. What was I supposed to say? Something positive, I guessed. I don't know if anyone understood me, but I told them that being a Christian does not guarantee a trouble-free life. It was important that in this time of grief we turned to God instead of running from Him. We needed to trust God, not question Him. We needed to allow God to heal us.

I really wanted to believe all that, but truthfully, it was more words than conviction. I guess that's what you get when you shove a microphone in the face of someone who has just suffered a tremendous loss and ask them to offer words of encouragement.

When the service ended, people came and greeted me. Some who could speak a little English tried to tell me something special about Jacob. Jake spent just one week with the people of San Luis Potosi, but he left a lasting impression. They experienced Jacob's loving nature and seemed deeply saddened by his death.

After the service, I was taken to the airport to meet a man and make arrangements to bring the cremains home. He escorted me to a private room where he demonstrated how to tape the boxes tightly closed and pack them into suitcases. At the airport I was to check the bags in with my other luggage and not make mention of what the suitcases contained. I felt like a drug smuggler, but I wanted out of Mexico and was willing to do whatever was necessary to bring the boys home.

Apparently, some good people were looking out for me. Later I would learn that an agent from the American Embassy demanded a fifteen-thousand-dollar payment before he would sign the papers authorizing the release of the bodies. If it had not been for sneaking around in the middle of the night to retrieve the cremains and smuggling them out in my luggage, I would not have been able to get them on the airplane.

We went back to Ruben's house where we taped the boxes closed and then packed them into two suitcases. If everything went as planned, I would be flying home the following evening.

Ruben's family was very kind to me. Their children brought out guitars and played songs for me. They took me to see a shopping mall that had a Sears store. Sears looked as out of place in Mexico as I did.

Mexico is full of Mexicans, nothing else. I stuck out like a sore thumb. People stared at me and that caused me to feel uncomfortable. Life is different there. Maybe I would have enjoyed it under different circumstances. Some people and places will always hold a warm place in my heart, and some experiences would be better forgotten if only I could.

Losing a child is very hard. People normally have plenty of support right at the beginning of the grieving process. My situation wasn't normal. I was alone in a strange land with no one to talk to. I was forced to talk to God, the same God who hadn't stopped this from happening. That was kind of like being forced to hug your sister after having a fight. It's not easy trusting in a God whose actions you can't understand.

I left Mexico that next evening. On the flight home we encountered the most beautiful thunderstorm I had ever seen. I never saw one streak of lighting, but witnessed the glow left behind the clouds. It was a peaceful storm, if there is such a thing. There was nothing to fear. It was as if God was telling me not to focus on the menacing lightning, but instead to concentrate on the beautiful glow it birthed. Jake was safe with Him. I might not understand how God could allow this horrid thing to happen, but I should be aware of the glorious result.

Well, that sounded good, didn't it? It would be nice to end the book right there. But how can I? You see, I thought I had come to some resolution on that plane ride home. But reality kept trying to break through my attempt at positive thinking: I'd been cheated.

I wanted Jacob back. I really liked having him tag along with me. I loved watching him grow. I cherished his friendship. Jake was the boy I always wanted to be. He was popular and good-looking. He was intelligent and talented. He played Little League Baseball and basketball. He joined me in most everything I did, whether it was carp shooting, ice fishing or nighttime raccoon hunting. Jake could use tools and liked to build things. All the skills my father taught me I was passing on to him. Jacob had wanted us to build a tree fort together in our willow. I'd promised him we would. We'd started making great plans, but it somehow kept getting put on the back burner. The tree fort never got built. My expectations for Jake's life never came to pass. Instead, he vanished from my life in a violent instant on that Mexican highway far from the arms of his father's protection.

Chapter 4

An Explanation Please

"Pain is unmasked, unmistakable evil; every man knows that something is wrong when he is being hurt... But pain insists upon being attended to..."[5]

~ C.S. Lewis

After everyone had patted me on the head and assured me Jake was in a better place, after all the cards had been read, after all the support had been given, I had to go home. I had to go on. I had to clean out his room.

Do you know how hard it is to dismantle the accumulations of a fourteen-year-old boy's life? What do I do with the rabbit's foot, the sea shells and the lucky coin key chain found with other treasures he kept hidden away in a cigar box? This stuff would ordinarily be junk, but now it seems so precious. How do I throw out anything with his handwriting on it? What do I do with the tooth found carefully stored in that cigar box? That tooth is the only thing I have left of him to hold.

Shortly after the funeral, people began to avoid mentioning Jacob's name. Some would even turn away when they saw me approaching. What they didn't realize was that I still wanted to hear and tell stories about him. Why couldn't they speak as if they remembered him? I surely remembered him! His dying shouldn't change the fact that he'd lived. He was a part of my life and would continue to be. Can't we talk about those who have died with the same enthusiasm we have for the living?

I could only force a smile for so long. I came to the realization that nothing had been resolved. You don't live with and love someone their entire life without having their death hurt. It's supposed to hurt! When you grieve, you find yourself set apart, distanced from others. Like a man with an unquenchable thirst, I longed for relief. How is it that some people are able to hold their heads up high and move forward while others struggle with loss? Was I wrong to want to continue licking my wounds? I never asked to be seen as an example of strength and the flag-bearer of faith.

There was too much emotion bottled up inside me to let it go, and I struggled to find a way to release it. That emotion built like steam pressure in a reservoir tank. It needed to be relieved before the tank exploded. Grieving necessitates some sort of safety relief valve. Occasionally, a little outside assistance is welcomed.

Author and lecturer Leo Buscaglia once talked about a contest he was asked to judge. The purpose of the contest was to find the most caring child. The winner was a four-year-old whose next-door neighbor was an elderly gentleman who had recently lost his wife. Upon seeing the man cry, the little boy went into the old gentleman's yard, climbed onto his lap, and just sat there. When his Mother asked what he had said to the neighbor, the little boy said, *"Nothing. I just helped him cry."*[6]

That little boy reminded me of Jacob. Jake was a deep thinker, always pondering the world around him. There were times it almost seemed he'd been here before. He was an old soul, wise beyond his years. He was the poster child for the biblical definition of love found in Corinthians 13:4–8:

Back to Tonic

"Love is patient, love is kind. It does not envy, it does not boast, it is not proud. It is not rude, it is not self-seeking, it is not easily angered, it keeps no record of wrongs. Love does not delight in evil but rejoices with the truth. It always protects, always trusts, always hopes, always perseveres. Love never fails."

Jake wasn't in a hurry; instead he was willing to pause and take note of what was taking place around him. I had an art teacher who asked me to look at a picture of a car and tell me how many colors I saw. I studied it and answered, *"four"*.

She said, *"I see eleven."* Then she said, *"Before you can learn to draw you need to learn to see."* Those words apply to almost everything in life, and Jake understood that.

Jacob accepted everyone. You didn't have to qualify for him to give you his attention. He just seemed able to make time for people. He was a popular kid with lots of friends but didn't limit himself to just the popular kids. He had enormous interest in people, even those others shunned. One of his teachers told us Jake would regularly skip recess to read to kids with special needs. Jake never mentioned that to us.

After the accident, one of his former elementary school teachers wrote us a note that further reflects his character:

"There was more to Jake than being smart...Jake

*understood humor, was responsible, reliable, sensitive,
creative – all things that a teacher doesn't forget. I
watched Jake grow and mature at Parkview. Mr. Blazek
and I would often talk about other students in the first
grade class, and our question would be, 'Think he'll be
another Jacob Kiepura?'"*[7]

~ *Pat Spalla*

Central Junior High School created a memorial award in
Jacob's name to the student who most excelled in computer
skills and also most exemplified Jake's good character. Some
twenty years later, they continue to present that award. There
are only a few teachers remaining who remember Jake. They
often cry through each year's ceremony. On two occasions,
the award was not presented because the teachers felt
strongly that no one in that class lived up to the legacy the
honor represented.

On Mother's Day the year after Jake's death, a young girl
called our house. She introduced herself as a student who had
attended the same school as Jake. She explained to Jan how
kids were cruel to her, constantly picking on her because she
wore leg braces. One day while they were teasing her Jacob
noticed them and came to her rescue. He confronted the
group on her behalf, and because of him the teasing stopped.
She told Jan she just wanted her to know she would never
forget Jacob Kiepura, and in his absence, she wanted to wish
her a happy Mother's Day.

Back to Tonic

Why would God allow a young man like Jacob to die when there was so much good he could have accomplished? Is it wrong to ask for an explanation? Was He looking the other way? Didn't He see it coming? A Loving God? What exactly does that mean? How could He have stood by and let this happen; especially to Jacob; especially to me?

The Book of Job is about a man of enormous wealth and goodness. He knew that he was a good man and probably felt that God was pleased with him.

I'm not a wealthy man, but I thought I was a fairly good man, a good father and husband. I thought God was happy with me. When all the trouble came upon Job he fell to the ground, worshiping God. Job understood God's authority; I probably didn't.

It's easy to thank God for your blessings when you have as many as Job had. But in the story, Job loses it all. He has nothing. He is broken. He is in shock. The loss is terrible. But I think there being no obvious reason for it all made it even harder on Job. That's what I was really struggling with.

Job's friends sat silently with him for seven days. But then they made the mistake of deciding to speak. They knew Job was a good man. They didn't understand God's motives, and they didn't want to suffer the same fate as Job. They started to accuse Job in an attempt to separate their lives from Job's.

Chapter 4: An Explanation Please

After all, if Job really was blameless and all this happened to him then what might become of them?

Job was in misery; angry with his friends and maybe angry with God for letting these dim-witted companions approach him. The last thing he needed was to have people giving him advice when they didn't know what they were talking about.

Job struggled with why this happened. He wished he had died at birth. That's interesting. Job didn't want his possessions back; instead he wished he were dead so he would never have had to live through this. It's as if he was acknowledging the will of God and just wished he didn't have to be a part of it.

I acknowledged that God was in control, but I had a hard time seeing Jake's death as part of God's will. I didn't wish I hadn't been born. However, I definitely wished I didn't have to live through this nightmare. I just wanted God to operate differently.

As the misery hung on, Job got more irritable. He felt he had a complaint, but decided to grin and bear it. When that didn't work he lashed out at God. He wanted someone to arbitrate between them. He felt that God had turned his back on him. He voiced his complaint to God. He felt cheated.

Job reached an impasse. He knew he couldn't move God. He was stuck in an earthly hell. He looked in all directions, but couldn't see God working anywhere.

Earthly hell was exactly what this felt like. I looked around me and saw nowhere to unburden my heart. Sadly, what many of my church friends seemed to really want was for me and my family to be strong for their sakes because the truth was, they were just as lost for answers as we were.

Trying to find comfort in the Bible, I became even more discouraged by the plight of Jeremiah, one of the most committed and enduring prophets of the Old Testament. Here was a man who answered God's call and did everything asked of him, yet he seemed to fail and struggle his entire life. I could relate to the intense feelings he expressed toward God.

> ### *Jeremiah's Complaint:*
> *"You deceived me, LORD, and I was deceived;*
> *you overpowered me and prevailed.*
> *I am ridiculed all day long;*
> *everyone mocks me.*
> *Whenever I speak, I cry out*
> *proclaiming violence and destruction.*
> *So the word of the LORD has brought me*
> *insult and reproach all day long.*
> *But if I say, 'I will not mention his word*
> *or speak anymore in his name,'*
> *his word is in my heart like a fire,*
> *a fire shut up in my bones.*
> *I am weary of holding it in;*
> *indeed, I cannot."*
> *~Jeremiah 20:7-10*

Chapter 4: An Explanation Please

Jeremiah thought God had promised him success and he felt betrayed. I can relate. I thought God promised me happiness, and it didn't turn out as expected.

Somehow Jeremiah was able to see beyond the struggles. My soul demanded rationalization. Maybe a day would come when I'd realize that God's promises were much different than my expectations, and His choices made perfect sense, but at this juncture, I was left only to ask: *Why?*

Chapter 5

Acts of Healing

"If you want happiness for an hour, take a nap. If you want happiness for a day, go fishing. If you want happiness for a year, inherit a fortune. If you want happiness for a lifetime, help somebody."[8]

~ *Chinese Proverb*

Back to Tonic

Living in the state of grief and depression I was in resembled existing in a detached dimension that ran adjacent to the world everyone else lived in. I felt more invisible than I did ignored. I had somehow acquired a cognitive disability that would not allow me to sense the sorrow in those who offered their sympathy. It was like eating a meal, but having no taste buds to benefit from the flavor.

People want to be available for their friends when they hurt. We feel obligated to come up with some kind of response, but unfortunately most have little to offer when it comes to healing. One person told me that I'd be *"blessed"* someday because of the accident. Blessed? How was I going to find a blessing in this? What kind of blessing could possibly be worth the loss of Jacob? Blessings aren't Band-Aids for tragedies.

It's possible that many people are just unaware of the magnitude of anguish one experiences when grieving, because, if they were aware, they most likely wouldn't say some of the dumb things they do at wakes. People mean well, but it's usually best to just keep your mouth shut. Many of our church friends struggled to find encouraging words. Continually telling me that everything happens for a reason didn't do much for me at that time. I needed something then, not in the future. One woman told Jan she was still young and could have another son.

Chapter 5: Acts of Healing

Really? We didn't want a different son, we wanted Jacob. I just wanted people to help me cry. I'm not good at crying. I needed someone to let me know they hurt along with me. I didn't want people to make sense out of what happened. Couldn't they just hold me for a moment... please?

I needed to know other people understood the enormity of my loss. I wanted to see and feel the pain in their faces. I wanted to hear the sorrow in their voices. I asked those who were closest to Jacob if they would mind putting down in writing how they felt when they learned of his death. That turned out to be an extremely beneficial experience, both emotionally and therapeutically.

A Letter from My Sister Joanne:
"On July 1st, 1992, I was busy around the house during the day. I remember going past my pantry door several times and finding it open, even though I don't remember opening it. It was a strange feeling. I also thought I heard music once, but the radio was not on. I remember thinking what a strange day it was.

When Ron came home from work we went outside to work in our rock garden. I had bought flowers that day to plant in it. It was about 7:00pm. I had just finished watering and I was dirt from head to toe. While shutting the water off at the back of the house, I heard the phone ring. I ran to the garage to answer the call. It was John. He said, "Jo, Jacob was killed in an accident in Mexico today." I remember trying to have to make sense out of what he was saying because it was so unbelievable it just wasn't registering with me.

I stood silent and remember John calling my name again, "Joanne, Joanne."

I started to scream, "Oh no, oh no. It can't be," and then I just screamed.

John said, "Jo, get Ron."

I called, and he came running; he thought I'd hurt myself. I handed him the phone, and John told Ron the details and then hung up. We both sobbed right there in the garage.

I remember saying, "I can't take this, I can't stand this, and God help us." I felt paralyzed and totally devastated. We must have cried for at least thirty minutes right there in the garage. Suddenly, rock gardens and new homes all seemed like silly, meaningless possessions, and I felt embarrassed to have ever been excited about them. Nothing mattered. A precious life had been lost. I just couldn't believe it.

I didn't know what to do. I looked at his picture on our fridge and I couldn't believe that I would never see Jacob

*again. I couldn't stop crying. It was at least an hour
before I could make a few phone calls..."*

Knowing that she and Ron felt pain to this intensity somehow
relieved me. I wasn't alone in this loss.

Joanne's letter continues...
*"...It was a long night and Ron and I left early Thursday
morning for Illinois. It was raining all the way. We
watched a storm front move in and we had to take cover
at a hotel because they put out a tornado warning. We
called Mom to let her know we'd be late, and she said
that you called and confirmed that Jacob was dead. We
really cried right there in the hotel lobby. All hope was
shattered. We felt helpless once again.*

*I'm grateful for our faith because at least I could pray
for you and your family. I felt like the storm was a
reflection of my state of mind...*

*...There isn't a day that goes by now that I don't look
at my rock garden and think of Jake. Sometimes I find
comfort in looking at it; sometimes I just feel pain."*[10]

Jacob and I loved storms. When storm warnings were issued,
the girls ran for cover while we ran outside. Few things
frighten us as adults, but storms display a sense of power
beyond our control. The authority of the wind scares me, yet
somehow I like it. It's not until a storm has caused you heavy

loss that you realize what a dreadful thing it can actually be. I never fully regained my love for storms after Jacob's death.

This was a dreadful time in the life of our family. It may have been selfish of me, but I really wanted to know people were still hurting. I needed to know people continued to experience the loss of Jacob. I received a number of letters similar to Joanne's. I would take them out at times just so I could taste the loss in the hearts of others. They have often been a source of release for me. If there is any such thing as *"magic words"* in times of great loss, it's those letters.

Actions of Love

I hate cemeteries and see no value in visiting them. There is nothing there for me. If I want to feel close to Jacob I go to the woods or the river or a baseball diamond. That's where we experienced life together. Cemeteries only affirm death. I don't know what you do at a cemetery. Jake's ashes are in the wall of a mausoleum. There are no flowers to plant or weeds to pull like we did when I was a kid on Memorial Day at my grandparents' graves. We just stand there and gaze at his name on the wall. After an uneasy half hour we leave, taking notice of countless other names on the walls and tombstones, names of people who are slowly and surely vanishing from the memory of people they once shared life with.

Initially, grieving families are flooded with attention, cards, meals, and prayers. Eventually, they become victims of everyone else's lives returning to normal—everyone's but theirs. We had to establish a new normal because life as we had known it didn't exist anymore. Every holiday, every anniversary tradition, every commonplace activity would be a new milestone to be faced without Jake.

For a grieving family, Christmas is an awful thing. When our kids were little, Christmas had been the most magical time of the year, not just for them, but also for Jan and me as we watched their excitement. Like many families, we had our seasonal traditions. Jan and the kids baked Christmas cookies together and I took them sledding down the huge hill not far from town. We'd decorate the house inside and out and made a big deal out of setting up our homemade manger scene. After attending the candlelight service on Christmas Eve, the girls would sleep with Jake in his room because it was closest to the Christmas tree. Spreading out their blankets on the floor against his door, they'd listen for Santa's arrival. One by one, they would take turns sneaking out to get a drink of water, go to the bathroom, ask a question... all the while hoping to catch the big man in action. It drove Jan and me nuts. I just kept wondering when they would finally fall asleep so we could put the presents under the tree and get some sleep of our own. Even when they were old enough to realize Santa wasn't real, just to keep tradition alive, just to be close to one another, they still sometimes slept together in Jake's room.

Back to Tonic

Every year we would display our special family decorations—crafts the kids had made and ornaments purchased to commemorate each passing year. Our tree top piece was a special tradition. One year we broke the angel that normally sat atop the tree. Jake suggested in its place putting part of the old broken Mickey Mouse lamp that once lit his toddler bedroom. After all, Mickey did have a perfect hole in his bottom where he was once attached to the lamp, and that would make him fit perfectly on top the tree. So Mickey became our permanent tree topper.

When the Christmas season following the accident arrived, we were hardly in a celebratory mood. I couldn't face the boxes full of memories. Every item down to that mouse had Jake's imprint on it. The thought of not hanging his stocking along with the girls' was just unbearable. Jan and I thought maybe we could buy a few gifts for the girls and go through the motions. As it was, the girls were just as uninterested in Christmas as we were.

My sister Arleen arranged to come over while we were out and decorate the inside of our house. She wanted to do something, and I'm sure she thought, *"How can they not have Christmas?"* We came home to find the house looking beautiful and realized just how much we needed that. It wasn't only the décor. It was the thought that Arleen stepped in and did for us what we couldn't find the motivation to do. I've always appreciated that my family never tried to offer advice. Instead, they offered actions and ears. They mourned alongside us.

At the gravesite we discovered that Jan's sister Ginger had left a fully-adorned mini-Christmas tree and garland decorating Jake's plot. I didn't know what to think. It was incredibly touching and extremely awkward. In the past, Christmas had been a festive season and the cemetery seemed to be an odd venue for a celebration. The Christmas tree looked so out of place. Nonetheless, the heart behind that gesture was so moving. I guess as much as I couldn't stand the idea of a Christmas without Jake she couldn't stand the idea of Jake without a Christmas.

Attempting to live on under the ever-present weight of Jake's death, the birth of a Savior became all the more significant. If there was any hope left it was the hope of the Gospel which appeared to be the only handhold in sight. I'd become a prisoner to promises of the God whom I'd felt already failed me.

Twelve Days of Christmas

Twelve days before Christmas we heard a knock on the door. We opened it to find a gift on the doorstep. There was a note attached: *"On the First Day of Christmas, Someone Gave to Me..."* This was repeated on each of the twelve days of Christmas. We tried to catch the person leaving the gifts, but they were tricky, coming at different times, day and night.

It wasn't the gifts or even the gesture that was so beneficial to us; it was the distraction. While wondering who would do such a thing and attempting to catch them in the act, our minds were, for a short time, taken off our sorrow.

We never caught the persons responsible, but we did learn a year later that it was the family of a girl that went to school with Cherie. That gesture left such an impact on our family that we have repeated it numerous times over the years for people who have also experienced a difficult loss. We have never been caught.

A Few Months Later:

Like my sister Joanne, my younger sister Arleen responded to my request to write down her emotions. She presented me with a letter I desperately needed to read. She wrote about how it was easier for her to talk with Jan because they are women and shared similar temperaments. Talking with me was harder for her. I recognized that it was largely due to my self-imposed isolation.

A Letter from Arleen:

"...There were times after Jacob's death when I would be at your house and you would come home from work. You would try to be cordial by talking a few minutes and then you would drift off into the living room. I would glance at you later and see you sitting on the loveseat all alone staring off into space. You were like an island isolated from the rest of us. The look of emptiness

on your face pierced my heart... I wanted to take some
of the pain away from you... I felt helpless... I had to
turn away from you so I wouldn't burst into tears. So
many times I wanted to come and sit with you and hug
you, but I thought if I did, it would make you cry, and I
didn't think you wanted to cry in front of me." [11]

Arleen was right; I didn't want her or anyone else watching me cry. It's a *"stupid thing,"* also known as a *"man thing."* I was fending off the best comfort available to me because of some innate sense of bravado. Some people called it being strong and demonstrating great faith. Calling it *"great faith"* instead of stubborn macho-ism was a lot easier to digest. Arleen's letter provided an image of me I needed to see.

Arleen could closely identify with my loss. Not only did she lose her dearly-loved nephew Jacob. She had experienced this type of loss before. Her best friend Janet, her soul-mate if you will, had been killed in a car crash. Arleen knew precisely what I was feeling. Jan had called Arleen the day of the accident and said, *"Arleen, I need you to come over here."* Not asking why, she immediately drove to our house.

Arleen recalled the day of the accident as her letter continued:

"...When I walked in the front door, Jan was standing
by the loveseat. It was obvious she had been crying. She
looked at me with sad eyes that seemed to be in disbelief
of what her mouth was saying, and in a slow, quiet

voice, Jan said, 'There's been an accident in Mexico.'
She paused for a moment, tilted her head, shrugged
her shoulders slightly and said, 'And they're all gone!' I
wanted to scream... As I grabbed Jan and held her I felt
like I was reliving Janet's death because the feelings were
exactly the same—horror, disbelief, pain, helplessness.
I remember trying not to scream because I had done
that on the phone with Jeff when he called me about
Janet and I realized that it made Jeff more hysterical. As
I held onto her tightly, I whispered in her ear, 'Are you
sure?'

"...I think the hardest part for me was when you came
home. You walked up to the door where Jan was
standing and you said in a half-question, half-statement
tone, 'It's Jake.' Then you hugged Jan. Then you said,
'What about the others?'... My heart was cracking into
a million pieces as I watched you being so strong on the
outside—knowing that you were dying on the inside...

"...I don't know when it will finally sink in. Life without
someone we love sometimes seems pointless. But we
must go on anyway..."[12]

"*Pointless.*" That perfectly described my view on life. There
seemed to be no point of "going on" without Jacob. Why
bother?

Chapter 5: Acts of Healing

Spring 1993

If you needed someone cradled, you wouldn't send my brother John. John has a very good heart, but the heart and the mouth didn't come as a matched set. John is a fixer; if he can't fix it, he doesn't know what else to do with it. So John did the only other thing he could think of; he introduced me to something he loved—golf. Golf was where he found escape from life's woes. He didn't just take me out for a day; he invested in me. He talked me into joining a league with him. You may not agree, but this is real help, real human help. John knew of no words that would repair my life, but wanted to do something, so he offered companionship. He offered an outlet. He made a personal commitment to just spending time with me. It is easier to offer almost anything other than time. Time is precious. Time is a sacrifice.

You don't have to be a minister or therapist to offer real help; you only need to demonstrate a willingness to show up. John showed up... John always shows up.[1]

---

[1] Isn't it interesting that the stories above about my sisters are long and emotional, while the story about my brother John is short and to the point? John's story is no less emotional or meaningful to me. I think it somehow is just another example of the differences between men and women.

Chapter 6

Nothing New Under the Sun

"The bitterest tears shed over graves are for words left unsaid and deeds left undone."[13]

~ Harriet Beecher Stowe

I don't know for sure if dogs grieve, but ours seemed to show signs of it at the start of the 1992 school year. Groups of kids could once again be seen walking past our house on their way to and from school. Sadie had seen this scene repeated many times before and it must have triggered an old ritual in her. She ran to our back gate where she had routinely waited for Jacob's homecoming in past years. Sadie stood there, tail wagging, anxiously anticipating his arrival. After twenty minutes or so the procession of school children ended, and she began to whimper. Moving about restlessly as dogs have a tendency to do when they crave something, Sadie waited at that gate for over an hour. For some time afterward, she would return to the gate, pacing back and forth, raising her nose into the air as if trying to locate her friend.

Like Sadie, I found myself very restless, anticipating something, but not knowing what. I caught myself running to the front door several times after hearing the slam of a car door. The sound caught me by surprise and that ember of hope still burning within me ignited the thought that it could have been them, returning from Mexico.

I felt handicapped, like a part of me was missing. It wasn't something visible like a severed leg or arm. I had lost my expectation. As time went on it never seemed to get better; it only became normal. The wound healed, but a scar remained. And while life went on, it did so much differently. I missed Jacob. I expected a long and happy relationship, and in a flash it was all gone. I grieved over the loss of the boy I knew, and

Chapter 6: Nothing New Under the Sun

the loss of the person he would become. Everything we had and everything we were supposed to have had been taken from me. I felt that both were owed to me.

My relationship with my grandfather was a similar experience. It ended too soon, actually, just as it was getting started. When I was a child, I never liked him. He seemed very hard and crabby. He and my grandmother lived next door to us. Their home was originally a chicken coup that was expanded into a three-room house. It was very small; one bedroom and no bathroom. They had an outhouse in the back. My mom and her three sisters were raised in that house. Our house wasn't much bigger, but at least it had an indoor toilet.

Grandpa was very demanding. Every holiday, he insisted his daughters and their entire families come to his house. It was probably only four-hundred square feet in total and was supposed to hold ten adults and thirteen grandchildren. Clearly, it was far too small for us all to fit inside, so we grandkids would have to sit outside in the driveway on the fenders of our parents' cars. When it was time to eat we would come in, grab a plate, stand against the wall, shovel it down and then head back out to the driveway. Perched on the fender of my dad's 1955 Chevy, I'd stare at my own house next door and think how much better it would have felt to be sitting on our couch right about then. Nevertheless, Grandpa wanted us at his place, so there we sat until the party was over.

Back to Tonic

At the age of fourteen, I found him to be an interesting person. I discovered we shared an interest in hunting, fishing, and pretty much all things outdoors. He told good stories about the old days. I liked the folklore approach he used as he spun his yarns. I had not realized we were so much alike.

Born in the late 1890s, he'd lived through many great events in history—the Wright Brothers' first flight, Henry Ford's production of the Model T, and Babe Ruth's major league debut. The *"Old Days"* came alive as he described life back then. I loved the story he told about the drunken pilot who would fly his biplane over town. Shouting from the cockpit, he'd offer rides to any young woman foolish enough to climb into his contraption. He'd then circle the area clipping the tops of the huge cottonwoods that covered the landscape. Grandpa's favorite pastimes included hunting rabbits and prairie chickens, and playing baseball.

Hard labor was no stranger to him. When he was young he'd worked in onion fields and moved houses with his father and brothers. Later he'd work in the stove works factory, the stone quarry and the steel mills. Now he was old and sick. Sugar diabetes, emphysema and arthritis had taken a toll on him. One afternoon I saw him standing along the road about a block from the house. He was leaning on his crutches and staring at the ground as if waiting for something to happen. I walked out to him. The pain in his legs and back had become too much for him and he couldn't go any further. I asked why he continued taking these walks. He said, *"If I don't keep trying, boy, I'll never walk again."*

He was tough; I think most men from his era were. I once saw my mom bringing ice over to his house. She told me he'd pulled a bad tooth earlier that day with a pair of pliers and he needed ice for the swelling.

He had been an alcoholic. After working the graveyard shift at the stone quarry, he and his boss would head to the local tavern. One particular night his boss was too intoxicated to drive home, so Grandpa grabbed the keys, stumbled his way into the driver's seat and took off down the road. Finding it hard to keep his eyes open, he drifted into a drunken slumber. He didn't see the freight train ahead at the crossing and rammed it broadside. The two drunken men were pulled into the moving equipment and down the track. His boss was killed; Grandpa survived. My mom told me the story when I was about ten years old and showed me the train crossing where it happened. Occasionally on those hot, sleepless summer nights I'd hear a train whistle moaning in the distance and I would try to imagine what it would have been like to be in that truck.

When I was sixteen, he died. I had gone to the hospital several times to visit him. The last time I saw him, he was—for the most part—quiet. I sat there with him for a while and then decided to leave. He grabbed my hand and squeezed it real tight. He wouldn't let go. He pulled me toward him and then he said, *"I love you, boy."* He had never said that to me before... I had never said that to him before. I don't know why, but it was hard to say. I wish I had said it more like I meant it.

The next day there was a phone call from the hospital. They needed someone from the family there right away. Being the only one home, I went. I found him alone. I walked into the room and went up to his bed. I asked him what was wrong. He didn't answer. I touched him and realized he was dead. As I looked at his body lying there, I was overcome with this feeling of missed opportunity. Our relationship had just begun. I'd finally gotten over my fear of him and learned to see him for the person he was. I'd wasted years I could have had with him. My mother always said he had a heart of gold, but I put off looking for it. Now he was gone and I would never get him back.

I guess I wanted to make up for missed opportunities with my grandfather by creating that special relationship early with my own children. I needed Jake to help me fill that void from the past. Now Jake was gone and I'd never get him back either.

There are certain people you just take for granted will always be in your life. It's a harsh reality to discover they won't.

Chapter 6: Nothing New Under the Sun

Ten years after my grandfather's death, I was overwhelmed by an unfamiliar emotion. While retelling one of his stories, I realized I'd forgotten a few of the details. No one else was familiar with his tale and he was no longer around to explain what took place. An empty feeling came over me as I realized that information was lost forever. In that instant I grasped the fearful reality of being left behind. The emotion caught me off guard and I never wanted to experience it again.

I saw that same emotion in Jacob one day. When he was around nine years old, I took him along with me to an area on the river I had not been to before. I wanted to check out the spot because I'd heard stories of walleye holes that produced good-sized fish. We parked alongside an abandoned railroad embankment. We had to hike a good way down to the river. As we walked away from the truck I got this premonition that I needed to tell Jake what he should do if something happened to me. So I explained to him that we were in an area where there was no one around and he would need to come back down to the road to wave down a passing car to ask for help. As I was speaking, I noticed his eyes welling up and realized I was scaring him. I was putting an enormous amount of responsibility on a boy who looked to me as his source of strength and protection.

I said, *"Jake, are you alright?"*

Trying not to show weakness, he swallowed hard and shook his head *yes*. But he meant no. I had looked at this as a teaching moment, but Jacob saw it from a perspective that he'd probably never considered before; his dad could die and leave him behind. I was just as important to him as he was to me.

"You know what?" I said. *"I don't feel like fishing anymore. How about you?"*

He shook his head no.

I said, *"How about we just go back to the truck and drive around out here in the country?"*

He shook his head yes.

Jake was quiet the rest of the day. He'd stare out the window and then every so often he would turn and stare at me. Mortality is a hard thing to ponder at nine years old.

It wasn't any easier at thirty-nine. With Jake dead and me a wreck, I opted to show strength instead of weakness. I decided I needed to strike out at someone. I contacted Illinois Senator Paul Simon and Congressman George Sangmeister about the actions of the American Embassy in Mexico. Congressman Sangmeister sent a representative to my house to interview me. With the information I provided, they launched a State Department investigation. While denying my claims of their failure to provide support and their attempts at extortion, the embassy had no proof to support their own claims. They argued that I refused all offers of assistance with lodging, transportation and communication. They denied demanding money and claimed I simply left before they could provide me with the documents necessary to leave the country with the bodies. As a result of that investigation, the ambassador was reprimanded.

The following January, a family from West Bend, Wisconsin, experienced a similar demand for money after losing five members of their family when a tour bus crashed into an electric pole and exploded. Twenty-five people in all were killed. Mexican officials delayed the release of bodies and demanded $15,000 before they would sign the necessary documents for their release.

I wrote Mr. Simon and Mr. Sangmeister and told them that, while I appreciated their efforts, it seemed nothing had changed in Mexico.

The world just didn't seem right. I could find no sense of fairness in it. I needed a sanctuary, someplace where I felt whole... in control.

Kankakee River
There's a special place on the Kankakee River where a large wooded island divides the water. Through the center of this island winds a small stream. The bank of that stream is lined

with Sycamore trees whose branches reach out over the water and conceal it from the rest of the world. Deer and raccoons find refuge under the canopy of that peaceful place. The stream contains several nice riffles and the fishing is good. To locate the area you have to wade out into the main river and work your way across the current to the piece of land that quietly splits the main channel. When you arrive at the island you're filled with a sensation of being in a different world. You're greeted by the jeweled elegance of the morning sun as it glistens off dew that collects on endless spider webs draping the area. Time seems to stand still. It is the perfect place for a father and son to grow together as friends. Jake and I claimed it as our own.

I decided to visit our secret sanctuary after Jake's accident. I expected something to be different about it, but it was just as it had been: beautiful. I thought maybe the trees and the fish beneath the riffles hadn't heard Jacob was killed, because if they had they surely would have displayed their sadness. But they didn't. They just continued to behave the same as they always had. I wondered how that place could remain so beautiful when I was so brokenhearted. What once produced a feeling of wonderment now offered only emptiness. How could it have abandoned me now; especially now? I left that place never wanting to return.

As I approached the main riverbank I saw a father attempting to teach his son to fish. They were wading, and I could tell they really didn't know what they were doing. I waved hello and asked how it was going. They said they weren't having any luck. They asked if I had caught any fish, so I showed them my stringer of rock bass. The boy's eyes lit up. The father asked me what I was using for bait. *"Spinners,"* I said. *"Just throw them in the slack water around the riffles."* I started to walk away but stopped. I paused for a moment and then turned to them and said, *"I know a place where you can catch some nice fish."* I led them to the island. As they waded into the source of the stream, I could see the same excitement on their faces that Jacob and I had experienced when we first discovered it.

They started to cast and before long the boy hooked a rock bass. The fish pulled hard against his rod and the boy anxiously reeled it in, fearing he would lose it. As he pulled the fish out of the water, he immediately brought it to his dad, smiling from ear to ear.

I realized my presence was no longer needed. I decided to leave the two of them alone to enjoy their time together. I wished them luck and, as I started to head out of that special place, I stopped, turned around, and asked the boy, *"What's your name?"*

He said, *"My name's Jake."*

Back to Tonic

"Generations come and generations go,
  but the earth remains forever.
The sun rises and the sun sets,
  and hurries back to where it rises.
The wind blows to the south
  and turns to the north;
round and round it goes,
  ever returning on its course.
All streams flow into the sea,
  yet the sea is never full.
To the place the streams come from,
  there they return again.
All things are wearisome,
  more than one can say.
The eye never has enough of seeing,
  nor the ear its fill of hearing.
What has been will be again,
  what has been done will be done again;
  there is nothing new under the sun.
Is there anything of which one can say,
  "Look! This is something new"?
It was here already, long ago;
  it was here before our time.
No one remembers the former generations,
  and even those yet to come
will not be remembered
  by those who follow them"

~Ecclesiastes 1:4-11

Chapter 6: Nothing New Under the Sun

I realized there was nothing all that unique about our father and son relationship. Our story would be repeated throughout the course of countless other father and son relationships, making our time together seem all the more meaningless. Jake and I appeared destined to be lost in life's shuffle.

With no prospect of a positive outcome on the horizon, and no new meaning of life yet revealed, it seemed the only thing left to do was to search for a clearer picture of God who gives life meaning.

PART II

"Sub-Dominant"

Chapter 7

The God I Thought I Knew

"You often meet your fate on the road you take to avoid it."[14]

~ Goldie Hawn

Several years passed. I had been trying to live up to the expectations of a church community that seemed to need me to be an example of faith. I talked about the strength and comfort I received from Christ and the peace I had in knowing that Jake was with God.

While in Mexico, I felt God's presence like never before and I thought that would help me pass through the stages of grief fairly quickly. It didn't. It just lingered on. It was then that I realized I was only pretending. The Bible no longer provided comfort. Its words seemed to have lost the influence they once had on me and I could no longer grasp the Being who expressed them. I wasn't sure I actually knew this God. The belief I strongly professed may have turned out to be something I never fully understood. That left me utterly humiliated.

Being humbled is, in a sense, like starting over. You need to go back and rebuild your confidence. It's best to rebuild on firmer ground using a foundation free of cracks and weak spots. That proved to be a slow and tiring process, but well worth pursuing if I didn't want to experience that same humiliation again.

I started at square one. I asked myself if I really believed God existed. I guess I'd believed that as long as I could remember. At the age of six, attending mass at our Catholic church, I hated to recite one particular reading. I don't know why; I just did. I believed that God lived in that gold box on the side altar where they kept the communion wafers. I thought if I hid behind the person sitting in front of me God wouldn't be able to see that I wasn't reciting the prayer. He was very real to me back then. As I grew older I still believed He existed, I just kind of fell into that comfortable belief that a merciful God wouldn't send people to hell. Heaven just wouldn't be as good as it could have been.

Jan had become a born-again believer before we met. When we started dating she invited me to join her church youth group activities. I agreed only because I was pursuing her, not God, and I figured the best way to stay in her favor was to act like I was really interested in *"finding Jesus."*

After we married we rented an apartment in my hometown. I promised we'd look for a church close by, but really I wasn't interested in finding one. We continued to meet with some of her friends in small group studies, but again, that was really only to make her happy.

We moved from our apartment into a house that we rented from the pastor of a local Bible Church. He was constantly inviting us to Sunday services and we did attend occasionally. Jan liked the church; I was just going through the motions.

The birth of our first child, Janene, changed me forever. In my arms lay this precious little creature that both melted my heart and caused me great anxiety. My sole purpose on earth had immediately become protecting her from harm. In my new role as father, I sought to guard her against all possible dangers. One event that was beyond my control was what would happen to her after death. That thought caused my renewed interest in God. I needed more than the light-some-candles-sprinkle-some-holy-water-God that I had been okay with in the past; I needed to establish some sort of relationship with this God whom I was going to entrust with my Janene's eternity.

Deciding not to play around with something as important as my daughter's wellbeing, I started attending church more regularly and earnestly sought after God. I searched the Bible for assurance. Beginning with the Book of John, I read, prayed, and read more. I began to understand the consequences of sins. A sense of vulnerability shrouded me as I recognized my own need of salvation. I remember the night I admitted my need of a savior.

Have you ever had one of those moments when you just completely drop your guard, just stop resisting? It was a cold January night with a full moon and cloudless sky. I was walking outside and kept looking up, asking for some clarity. I said, *"How do I do this? How do I know you're up there?"*

It was like the scene from the movie *Close Encounters of the Third Kind*. Richard Dreyfuss is sitting in his truck and suddenly he is engulfed in light. The truck begins to shake and he realizes that something strange is happening to him... Well, I wasn't engulfed in light or shaken off my feet, but I recognized something was happening to me. I experienced the presence of God that night in a different way, and I wanted more of it. I kept reading the Bible and several months later I was baptized. The predicament with becoming *"born again"* is that God's redemption happens in an instant, but it takes a lifetime to understand it and the God who made it possible.

To answer my earlier question; yes, I believed God existed. Running from Him would be a pointless endeavor; where was I to run? On to square two.

Was I wrong to believe that God looked after his followers? Losing Jacob was very painful, but there was so much more to it. What about the way God treated me? Why did God let this happen? He knew how much this would hurt me. I knew He could have stopped it. Why did it have to be so brutal? Why did they have to get robbed? Why did I have to smuggle the bodies out of Mexico? The Bible tells us God is a jealous god. Did I love Jake more than God? Was God jealous of that?

Why did I experience night terrors and visions, often waking in the middle of the night to the sound of my own uncontrollable shrieks? I'd be in a panic, believing the boys' mutilated bodies were pulsating there next to me. Lifting the covers with my hands plastered in their still-warm blood, I'd scramble to stop Jake's bleeding. Then Jan's voice calling, *"Honey, are you alright?"* would draw me out of the horror.

Other nights I'd seem to wake to find my bedroom crowded with strangers. The room would be illuminated with a dim grayish-blue light. These people would be sitting on my bed and dressers or standing at my bedside. They'd all be mumbling something, a quiet chant. It seemed as if some sort of meeting was going on about my fate.

Horrors such as these became so real I could not distinguish between dreams and reality. I would see things I knew weren't there. Early one morning while deer hunting I had an eerie encounter. After walking out to my stand in the dark I settled down and waited for dawn. At first light, I noticed a shape about twenty yards away. It looked like the figure of a person sitting against a tree. I would have heard another hunter walking into the area and I was certain if he had been sitting there when I arrived he would have said something. The woods still being fairly dark, I leaned forward, straining my eyes for a better view.

It was Jake.

He was sitting there in his camouflage just as he had so many times before. Turning away and rubbing my eyes had no effect; he was still there when I looked back. I knew it couldn't be him, but I wanted so badly to believe it was.

I could feel my heart thumping hard within my chest. Each new breath became increasingly more difficult to draw.

Chapter 7: The God I Thought I Knew

Remaining motionless there in my tree-stand, I attempted to process what was taking place. Finally, I said, *"He's dead. That can't be him."* At that point the figure slowly began to turn toward me. Its face morphed from looking like Jacob into a repulsive evil spirit. It began to rotate in a swirling mist and disappeared into a knothole of the tree like a genie returning to its bottle.

Had I just seen a demon? Was I going insane? Those types of terrors continued for some time. I couldn't help wondering what kind of merciful and loving God allowed things like that to happen.

Where was I to go from there? Who could I talk with about these dreams and visions? Certainly not my pastor; he also lost his son in the accident, but was unfortunately suffering from his own self-imposed state of denial. He claimed to have completely mourned the loss of Stephen during an eight-hour car ride home from Kentucky. I just could not fathom that anyone could *"grieve out"* in eight hours.

People at church pointed to all the positive things that came out of the accident. They didn't want to hear about this dark side of it. I couldn't bear to further burden Jan. She was aware of the nightmares because she experienced me waking from them, but I downplayed their effects on me. There were many things I didn't tell her about Mexico because I didn't want her to experience what I saw. I wanted to shield her from all of that, and all of what I was going through at the current time. We'd talk and share our heartache, but I just couldn't show weakness when my family needed strength. So where was the God I thought I had come to know? Where would I find strength? Would He send someone to help me?

Our church was made up of many good people. They wanted to offer comfort. But either they didn't know how or they didn't know how badly I needed it. We'd lost our mission team. The families of those boys were hurting and needed some kind of relief, but our pastor's emphasis was on making the whole ordeal sound like it was for some good purpose. I was made to feel that admitting I was having a hard time would be deemed sacrilegious.

Once, attempting to express my struggles, I referred to the accident as a tragedy.

A woman replied, *"Do you really think of it as a tragedy?"*

I was staggered by that comment. I felt like screaming, *"Yes, of course it's a tragedy! What the hell is wrong with you?"*

Instead I just sat there, mouth open, envisioning choking the life out of her.

While it was a tragedy for some of us, others found it to be an overbearing presence that always needed to be reckoned with and they preferred to just move on.

Chapter 7: The God I Thought I Knew

I didn't go down to Mexico just to retrieve my son; I brought back our mission team. I was the one who stood in the place of this church. I did all the dirty work. I experienced the horror for them. I took on the complete load. I stayed there in Mexico by myself and did the difficult things, and now that I needed help our church couldn't give it. Maybe it was because they couldn't admit the God they thought they knew wasn't the God He turned out to be. Some warned, *"Stay away from Gene or you'll be questioning your faith."* Was I doubting my faith or trying to understand it?

I often felt I was clinging to the rear bumper of the church bus as it sped down the road. I didn't know what was going on inside, nor could I see where it was going. It was exhausting. Many times feeling like an alien, I wondered if there was such a thing as election and I wasn't included. I'd seen men whose wives were divorcing them go through similar emotions. They loved someone who just didn't love them back, forever excluded from the life they wanted to be a part of. This might just fit. Why else would a loving and merciful God allow so much pain? Why was it seemingly just me going through this? Could it be that a loving and merciful God only took care of those He loved, and I wasn't included?

But I wanted God. Where did that leave me? I decided I had no other choice than to beat this thing. There was no other option. Somehow, some way, I had to hang around in God's shadow until I could work it out. I hid everything inside. I wouldn't reveal to anyone I was suffering. I was so successful I even convinced myself.

Satan uses doubt, weakness, and failure to his advantage. I never was a model Christian. I'd always been a bit of an outsider. When I started attending church regularly I thought the people were nice, but I wouldn't want to hang out with them. On the outside was where I now found myself. Satan is *"the accuser."* He did a good job of highlighting my failures and causing me to ask myself why God would want me. I didn't doubt there was a God, but I began to wonder if salvation really was an option for me.

I ran. I ran from that church. Division was starting as people began taking sides, recognizing the friction between the pastor and me. Feeling I was already on God's bad side for some reason, I certainly didn't want to make matters worse by dividing a church. To hide, we relocated to Deer Creek Christian Church. I'm not sure what we were hiding from, but we hid. I didn't want to get involved in anything because I was afraid people at DCCC would see me for what I really was. I was playing a role.

Cherie, our youngest daughter, is a talented actor. She must get her acting abilities from me, because I should have gotten an academy award for my performance at the new church. I knew all the right things to say. I could comment on the meaning of Bible verses and sound like I knew what I was talking about.

Chapter 7: The God I Thought I Knew

I really was living a life of two different personalities; one who fervently believed in and loved God and one who didn't know what to think. My life had turned into a big debate in which I argued both sides of the issue. How could a man who had experienced God as closely as I had now find himself this screwed up?

I had people tell me, *"Everything happens for a reason."* I didn't need philosophy; I needed help. Hoping someday far in the future to find the *"reason it happened"* just didn't console me at that terrible moment of my life. Those are not words of comfort. It's what people say when they don't know what else to say. Think about it: a man believing that to be true would then be sentenced to a desperate search lasting the rest of his life to find a reason good enough to justify his loss. Let me ask you this: What would you be willing to exchange for the life of your son? Sometimes there are no reasons; it just happens. If everything did happen for a reason there would be no such thing as free will.

I've listened to people go on about how they had been blessed by the Lord. God made a traffic light stay green just for them. He saved them a parking space right up front. They credit any favorable thing that happens as a blessing put upon them by God. I'm not saying it doesn't happen. I'm sure it does. But somewhere those claims lost traction when I compared their trivial green light to my tragic loss. Using petty triumphs to demonstrate the hand of God Almighty did more to diminish His purpose and influence than offer hope.

I wasn't looking for preferred parking. I was clinging to the face of a rock wall seeking a solid handhold. Their coincidental evidence led me to the conclusion that they had never experienced God in real desperation. They knew from nothing. Never having been pushed to the edge of their faith, their green light victories just didn't seem to cut it.

"Before you can draw, you need to learn to see."

Chapter 8

Healthy Anger

"Bitterness is like cancer. It eats upon the host. But anger is like fire. It burns it all clean."[15]

~ *Maya Angelou*

Jake and his childhood buddy Jason were best friends. Jason was a really neat kid who loved airplanes and Star Wars. The movie Star Wars debuted on May 26, 1977, exactly one year before Jake was born. Those two boys grew up in all the Star Wars hype and were constantly shooting down some imaginary enemy ship, sometimes turning their weapons on each other in heated battle.

One afternoon Jan walked up on me as I stood at the kitchen sink looking out the window. Asking what I was looking at, I told her that Jake and Jason were fighting in the backyard. They weren't just fighting; they were locked in mortal combat over a paper watch Janene had made for Jacob. Jan howled, *"What's the matter with you? Go out there and stop them."* Mothers sometimes don't understand that it's good for boys to test themselves. Boys need to learn to *"show up,"* to take a stand and defend their stuff... to see what they're made of. Reluctantly, I walked out there and pulled them apart.

Perhaps the time had come for me to show up; time for me to see what I was really made of. Maybe my approach to the accident and all that followed had been more from a defensive stance. It was time to play offense. But there was no way I could do it alone. I really needed to find someone who could come alongside me and walk me out of this depression.

On a TV program, I once heard the story told of a man who fell into a pit and was trapped. A doctor walking by heard the man calling for help.

Chapter 8: Healthy Anger

The man in the pit shouted, *"I'm trapped down here. Can you help me?"*

The doctor said he could and wrote him a prescription for something to settle his nerves, dropped it in the pit, and walked on.

Next a preacher answered his call for help by reading several soothing Bible verses to comfort his soul. He also walked on.

Finally, a third man, hearing his cries, jumped down into the pit.

The confused man in the pit asked, *"Why did you do that? Now we're both trapped down here."*

He replied, *"No, we're not trapped. I've been here before, and I know the way out."*

Could there be someone out there capable of showing me the way out? I had yet to find that person. I was somewhat reluctant to talk to Earl, my new pastor, about what I was going through. I was afraid of getting the same old standby Christian response, *"Trust God... He's in control."* But Earl was a good guy, so I started relating bits and pieces just to see how he'd respond.

Earl told me he had just met someone who may possibly be able to relate. Cautiously, I agreed to talk with this person. So I went to church one evening to meet with this *"expert."*

Back to Tonic

I was waiting in the church office when a woman came to the door. I got up to see if I could help her. She introduced herself and said she was looking for Gene. My blood pressure elevated. I never pictured the person jumping into the pit with me as a middle-aged African-American woman. I was skeptical and wondered how this woman was going to be able to relate to me.

The skepticism quickly vanished. After a short introduction, she got right at it. She didn't offer answers; instead she asked some poignant questions that could only come from someone who had experienced not only my heartache, but also my frustration. She understood the tension, the queasiness, and the melancholy I'd been dealing with. It was like acupuncture therapy. She knew where to place each needle and as she did there was a sense of temporary relief.

Her questions served to earn my trust, and sensing that, she asked me to tell my story. She just sat and listened for an hour without saying a word. I couldn't stop talking. Emotions gushed out of me like water from an open hydrant. When I finished, she astonished me by repeating the story back to me. She'd heard me—actually listened to me. She made no attempt to fix anything. She just let me unload. After highlighting several areas of the story that seemed to jump out at her, she related a few things from her own life that would qualify her to understand my feelings.

Chapter 8: Healthy Anger

She didn't offer answers. Instead, she proposed a new perspective on things. Saying I needed to do something for myself first, she gave me an assignment. She asked me to go home and make a list of all the people I was angry with. I told her I wasn't angry.

"Yes, you are," she said. *"Now go home, pray about this, and bring me back a list next week."*

After some intense prayer, I jotted down the first transgression:

I was angry with Juan for not protecting my son.

Writing that down felt good. I hadn't realized I carried that feeling of resentment. I didn't want to be angry with him.

After that, the list became easier to compile. Like opening an old water spigot that had been rusted closed for years, complaints began to gush out of me, complaints I didn't know I harbored.

My list:

> *I'm angry:*
> a. *At Juan for not protecting my son.*
> b. *Because my son died in a place where he was a stranger.*
> c. *Because they treated him like just another body.*

d. *Because he was robbed.*

e. *Because their things had been looted.*

f. *Because I don't see anything positive coming from it.*

g. *Because I didn't touch him.*

h. *Because Jan couldn't be with him.*

i. *Because my girls only got to see a box of ashes.*

j. *Because some people in Mexico and our embassy saw the accident as a way of making money.*

k. *Because no one ever thanked me for staying behind and seeing to it that the remains of their loved ones returned home.*

l. *Because people thought it was okay for me to be the one to identify the bodies, saving them from the horror.*

m. *Because my pastor told me I was wrong to lie on the phone and say I was him in order to get his son's body released.*

n. *Because I wasn't allowed to mourn.*

o. *Because I didn't like the way funeral services were handled.*

p. *Because of the problems that arose in church afterward.*

q. *Because our pastor persuaded us to use the memorial fund to fix up the church.*

r. *Because our pastor seemed to just want to sweep the whole experience under the carpet.*

s. *Because we had to leave the church.*

t. *Because I was looked at as the bad guy.*

u. *Because God didn't put someone in my life to help me through this.*

v. Because God didn't stop it.

w. Because my dreams were shattered.

x. Because of the nightmares.

y. Because I don't understand.

z. Because of the pain it caused my family.

aa. Because I miss him.

bb. Because I feel isolated.

cc. Because I have little tolerance for people who don't know what they are talking about.

dd. Because I allowed myself to get to this point.

ee. Because I'm spiritually lazy.

ff. Because I'm not sure what I want.

gg. Because people look at me as some kind of an example.

hh. Because people think I know what to say to someone suffering a loss.

ii. Because my heart's desire always has been to have a son.

jj. Because I can't remember what he looked like.

kk. Because nothing changed.

ll. Because everything changed.

She was right. I was angry; angry about a lot of things. The amazing part of it was that as I wrote each item down I found myself letting some of that anger go.

For over eight years I had viewed my world through the window of Jake's death. I couldn't enjoy one moment of his life or our relationship without also seeing him as dead. I was continually haunted by the memory of him lying there looking as if he had just gone through some exhausting physical exertion. His hair was a mess and looked as if sweat had dried and left it glued awkwardly to the side of his head. He was bruised and covered with small cuts. His face was swollen and he had huge wounds at his neck and elsewhere on his body. Dirt and dry blood were spattered about his entire body. The expression on his face wasn't the look of being at peace like I kept telling myself. It was one of him knowing something that I didn't know, along with a trace of an expression that seemed to be saying: Where were you?

I needed to add one more item to my list. I was angry with myself for letting this happen to him. I'm a protector. I'm a fixer. I couldn't help believing if I had been driving that van that morning none of this would have happened. I was stuck in a rut where I kept kicking myself for failing him. For me, looking forward involved staring over the body of my son, whom I had failed to protect.

This woman explained to me that I needed a reverse perspective. I needed to find a way to see the world from his life forward instead of his death backward. She said that perspective would change the way I would see everything else.

I found that hard to do on my own. I was going to need to rely on help from others, and I had never been the type of person who readily relied on other people.

Chapter 8: Healthy Anger

It may be easier in times of grief to babble to strangers than to family or friends because there's no history for them to deal with. It just is what it is. Strangers are not emotionally attached to your loss; they are not dealing with their own grief. It seems you can pass off a little of your emotion on them.

It's like carrying around a bucket full of water. It's heavy and we long for some of it to be taken from us. Family and friends come to help, but their buckets are also nearly full. Strangers come with room in their buckets, so you unload a little on them and lighten your burden a bit.

I've encountered a few special people I just loved being around. One of them is Pat. She's a lovely person who co-led the worship team at our new church. Pat saw value in me when I saw none. She pursued me—pretty much forced me—to play bass guitar for our church band. She got me to take my mind off my misery. She never gave advice about my situation; she created a new situation for me to spend time thinking about, all the while acknowledging my right to mourn.

And then there was Pat's partner in crime, Kelly. Everybody needs a little Kelly. She's the peanuts in the box of Cracker Jacks. I can't explain what she does, but you find yourself savoring every moment she's around. She is a spiritual giant with the genuine quality of caring about people. She leaves you feeling like you are a blessing to her, like you're something special. She just makes me smile and I feel safe in her company.

Pat and Kelly were some of God's best—my personal angels. I was surrounded by many other good people, but the friendship of these two women marked a turning point in my journey. Through them I was able to share bits of Jacob's life. They were a breath of fresh air... and I had been waiting to exhale for a long time.

"What moves through us is a silence, a quiet sadness, a longing for one more day, one more word, one more touch, we may not understand why you left this earth so soon, or why you left before we were ready to say good-bye, but little by little, we begin to remember not just that you died, but that you lived. And that your life gave us memories too beautiful to forget."

~ *(Author Unknown)*

Chapter 9

Jake's Mexico

"I found a toilet with a real seat. I was so happy."

~ Jacob

Mexico could have been remembered for things other than the accident. Jake was the youngest of the boys on the trip, but his size and maturity would have make you believe he was older than fourteen. As he was part boy and part man, the wonderment of this foreign place must have been awe-inspiring to him. I wish I could have seen the excitement in his eyes as he experienced this new culture. He said that seeing these poor people made him appreciate how much he had at home. He talked about how much he liked San Luis Potosi and wanted to return someday to live there for a year or more.

Had he returned home alive from this trip, we would all have been taking pleasure in his stories, photographs and keepsakes. The impact of this kind of trip on a young boy visiting a third-world nation is usually life changing.

Jacob did enjoy his experience in Mexico. I believe he would have returned with greater compassion than he possessed when he left home. I'm certain he would have matured a great deal as a result of the trip, but he was still a boy and a lot of Mexico was seen through the eyes of a boy coming of age.

In spite of the hellish nightmare digging through the blood-soaked van, I'm incredibly grateful to have recovered his journal. It is my one window into the last weeks of his life here on earth.

Jake may have been in the same poor country I was in, but his Mexico was a bit different from mine.

Chapter 9: Jake's Mexico

Jake's log:

"We saw an accident. It looked like a blazer ran into the back of a semi. The blazer was literally crushed.

"Mexico wasn't all that bad. As far as litter goes, it's not bad. There is an abundance of dirt. There are palm trees and cacti and plenty of other exotic plants... After a while you could see the mountains. We went on a toll road so that we could go through the mountains. They were beautiful and after that the mountains never left our sight.

"Finally we reached Vanegas. That is a small town near Tanque. Juan asked about twenty people for directions. About five of them were right. From Vanegas we got on a dirt road. It was awful. There was a good road right next to the one we were on but there were big rocks laid across it. The road was very bumpy and dusty. The car is filthy. We went about 23km when we reached a town. Juan asked directions and we had to go another 22km. About half way down the <u>trail</u>, we saw a car. Juan stopped and blinked his lights. The car stopped and four men came out. It was the pastor and three villagers. Everyone was happy. So we went to the church. We met some people, and then we hung our hammocks and went to sleep. It was freezing and to top it off I was by a window with a screen."

Once during the trip when Jacob was able to call home he told us all about how he was reading his Bible when a goat came up and started eating the hammock where he was laying.

"In the morning the roosters were crowing like crazy. We took a small tour of the town. It was very interesting. We saw women grind corn, men branding cows, and many other things. After that we had a Bible study. Then we played volley ball. A little later we went for a walk. We walked about five miles. We circled a lake, rode mules, climbed a small mountain, and plenty of other things. I forgot to put sun screen on and I got a horrible sunburn. Then we played more sports and had a service."

The boys started their mission trip at Tanque de Delores. Jake wrote about climbing a small mountain. This is where we believe he took a picture of a cross with a wreath around it. People used to crawl up the side of the mountain and offer sacrifices to God at this cross.

The boys helped a doctor that came to Tanque give free medical assistance to the people. They cleaned instruments, gave medication and bandaged patients. One of the boys had to hold a woman's tongue while the doctor cut off a growth.

The boys also helped four girls that came to Tanque from San Luis Potosi conduct a Vacation Bible School. One of the girls said Jacob understood Spanish very well; and that he liked to drink Coke.

Chapter 9: Jake's Mexico

Jacob acted like a clown and got the children laughing during the Bible school. At one point, Jake was supposed to be holding the music sheets for the other boys to read as they played their instruments, but Jake decided to dance around with them instead. He kept pulling them away from the other two boys and everyone was having a good laugh.

Before crossing the Mexican border they spent $600 on supplies that they gave to the people in Tanque, including clothing, personal care products, and toys. The people had very little food, so Juan and the boys gave away most of what they had brought for themselves. For more than a day, they themselves went without food and, if you've ever been around hungry teenaged boys, you know what a feat that was.

When we talked to Jake from Mexico City he talked about how the others didn't like the town of Tanque because it was so harsh and primitive, but he thought it was neat because it reminded him of where he and I went hunting.

He said to those people, church was everything and the service lasted all day.

After that, they left Tanque and headed for the city of San Luis Potosi. There were quite a few girls their age and they all seemed to like that. The boys worked with the church there in their outreach to the city where they challenged other boys to sports competition.

Back to Tonic

"In the morning we got up and went to church to meet some of the youth group and see the town. We sang our songs and it all went pretty well. From there we went to Tangamango. It is a huge park. I'd say it was 5 sq. miles. We went and played basketball, and then we ate. The food was very good. Then we played volleyball. After that they decided to have a church service there rather than go back to the church. Later, about 8:00, we went to the plaza again. We were supposed to see some concert but the person never showed up. So we walked around for awhile.

"Juan asked two other boys to come along with us. Now there are seven people in the van."

The pastor there had a young boy named Jonathan. He was about eight years old. Jacob had a good time with him. They became good friends and Jake played around with him quite a bit. Jake would pick him up and say, *"I'm taking him with me."*

The pastor said that Jacob had a special quality; he was always very warm and friendly. He said that each morning Jake would go downstairs to the pastor and his wife and greet them by saying, *"Good morning."* After breakfast, Jake would put his hand on the pastor's shoulder and thank him for the food and tell them how good it was. Then he would pick up his dirty dishes, bring them to the sink, and wash them. This really impressed the pastor.

Chapter 9: Jake's Mexico

He said that Jake was always ready to help and was a pleasure to have around. Jake had the ability to make others feel good and had left a lasting impression on the people.

From there the seven of them moved on to San Miguel and Salamanca:

"We piled into the car after we said good-bye to everyone. It was sad. We went about 3 hours. We sang songs to Sam playing the guitar. We stopped in San Miguel. We looked in some <u>huge</u> churches. There were little statues that people would worship. There was about $3 million worth of gold there. We also saw a dead guy from the first century. Then we walked about sightseeing. Then we went to Salamanca. We stayed at Juan's relatives' house. We saw a roach about two inches big. This morning we woke up early as usual. We can't go to Mexico City yet because the pastor can't drive on Wednesdays. (Due to the heavy pollution there, people are only allowed to drive on designated days).

"We went to the fair and while we were there we saw some little kids with bags of flour that they were throwing at people. Being the day that John baptized Jesus, it's a custom to throw water and flour at people. The kids saw that we were American and they decided to chase us. We ran into a church court yard and I even ran into a women's house but the kids kept following us and throwing flour. I went at a kid with my fist clenched

but he just threw flour in my face. So I broke from the group and ran until I thought I was safe. Then I felt a tap on my arm and I turned around to get more flour in my face. So I ran and hid behind the foosball tables. I was like a ghost. It took forever to get the flour off. Then I saw the others and went to them. Within a few minutes the kids came again and chased us. One kid ran out of flour and started throwing dirt, and to top that off, when they were done they asked for money.

"*There was a lady selling taped egg shells filled with confetti. They were a blast. Jake had his shirt tucked in so I cracked one in his shirt. Later I did the same to Sam, only, (which I wasn't aware of); the egg was filled with flour. It was hilarious.*"

From there they moved on to Mexico City.

"*We went about three hours when we found the pastor. He led us back to the church. You wouldn't know it was a church if you passed it on a road. We got there, unpacked, and started to work right away. We dug a trench and a large spot for the trench and two others to meet. We put a large pipe in the trench and mixed cement to fill it back up. After that we started painting a room.*

Then when we finished for the day, Sam, Hector, and Steve went to a relative of Sam's house. Jake, Brian,

Chapter 9: Jake's Mexico

and I tried to get our own hotel room. After that failed
we went to the roof and talked about the paint job
we're going to get on our car. Then we went to sleep in
the van. We got about seven hours of sleep when Juan
woke us up. We ate breakfast just before 9:00 then went
straight to work. We mixed more cement, hauled three
large piles of dirt and rock out to the front, dug two
more trenches, put in one more pipe, chiseled a cement
block for the other pipe, and built a ceiling support.
Steve, Sam, and Hector showed up about noon, we were
angry. Afterwards we went to play soccer with some
people at the church. We were against a team of drug
addicts. We lost 8 to ten; we all made some good plays.
Then we passed out tracts." [16]

One very special keepsake came from a girl named Areli that Jacob had met in Mexico City. She was 15 years old and the sister-in-law of the pastor from the church there. Stephen wrote in his journal that Jacob and Areli walked around the city together all day long and by the end of the day they were together. We found a note in Jacob's wallet from Areli. It read, (in broken English),

"HELLO, I WILL GIVE YOU TIP. I LIKE YOU A LOT.
I AM GLAD TO MEED YOU. ARELI"

We received a letter written in Spanish from Areli a few weeks after the accident. Jacob's Spanish language teacher translated it for us.

Back to Tonic

"To the Family of Jacob Kiepura,
I hope that in these terrible times that are passing that
you are materially and spiritually well, but most of all
that you receive help from God.

I don't want to be a nuisance or a bother but I would
like to ask a favor of you. I would like to have a picture
of your son Jacob. I asked him for one while we were
together in Mexico City but he didn't have one with
him.

I don't know how you are going to take this but I feel
that I need to tell you that I was Jacob's girlfriend while
he was here.

He is my first boyfriend and I say is because he still lives
in me. I am not able to forget him because he not only
helped me very much spiritually but he also made me
feel some things that I had never felt before.

I am a Christian and my name is Areli and I live
in Cordoba Vera Cruz. I met Jacob while I was on
vacation in Mexico City visiting my sister. She told me
of this young man full of the Spirit of God, full of love,
polite, and well mannered, with a great desire to become
a missionary. My sister is the wife of the pastor from
Mexico City.

I don't know if he was like you, but if he was, you would
be full of compassion and maternal love, and have the
spirit of service that Jacob had.

Chapter 9: Jake's Mexico

If you will permit me to confess, I am afraid to love someone as I loved your son because it hurts so much to lose them. Just two months before I met Jacob my sister's daughter died. I was still recovering from this loss and now I have lost Jacob in the accident.

I don't know if there is any reason to live. I don't understand the things that have passed. They fill me with pain and sadness. They blotch out the dreams of the future. You question what is worth living for.

I begin to hate the truck driver because what he had done was so offensive. I hate the road where the accident happened.

It was a great tragedy because they served God with all their hearts. You question why God would let this happen.

Forgive me for writing what I feel. I must stop writing now or I will never stop. I want so much to have a picture of Jacob.

He will always be with me. It hurts and has greatly affected my heart so much because I loved him so much.

Please write me in English because I have someone who can translate for me. I hope that you have found someone to translate this letter for you.
From one who will always love your son,[17]
Areli"

We sent her the picture of Jake she requested, along with a letter from us. We wanted more... so much more. We were dying to know anything Jake did or said, and we'd loved to have learned about his romantic encounter. She never wrote back.

His journal ends at Mexico City. He told us on the phone that they were talking about going to Acapulco for a day or two after they had finished their work in Mexico City because they wanted to see as much of Mexico as they could while they were there. He wanted to know if we would be mad at him if he went to Acapulco...

Information from that point on was provided by Hector, the lone survivor. Their van was broken into while they swam in Acapulco Bay. Personal items bought on the trip were taken. The film we recovered showed them enjoying the beach on what would turn out to be their last full day on earth. We know little more, they were killed outside of San Luis De La Pas on their way back from Acapulco.

Beyond the grief of losing my son, beyond the torment of my night terrors, beyond the feeling of utter abandonment and exile from God, there was something else I just couldn't swallow. As irreverent as this may sound, if God had been standing before me I would have liked to have grabbed Him by the shoulders and vehemently shook Him shouting, *"Don't you get it?! These boys were living for YOU! They were gifted and passionate and dedicated to your cause! They were loving and serving and humble! What were you thinking? These boys would have made a huge impact for your kingdom and you just deleted their existence from the face of the earth."*

I poured over that journal, imagining their experiences as best I could, trying to see the good that could be taken from this. But the only conclusion I could draw was that God's so-called perfect plan was idiotic.

Chapter: 10

Hey God

"A lie can travel half way around the world while the truth is putting on its shoes."[18]

~ *Charles Spurgeon*

I once took Jacob to a father and son prayer breakfast. After we had eaten we all went into a prayer time. One by one I could hear the leaders of the church take their turns at prayer. Unexpectedly, I heard Jake begin to pray. He didn't pray like a kid. He prayed as if he actually knew who he was talking to, as if he was picking up a conversation from where it left off the day before. The heart of his prayer demonstrated an ongoing relationship with God. I was humbled, so humbled that I couldn't even find it in myself to be proud. I came to believe that this boy was somehow destined to make a difference.

After the accident, my level of faith slowly dissipated. I came to the point of there being a huge difference between what I accepted as true in my mind and what I actually believed in my heart. Once having the kind of Godly relationship my son demonstrated, I now was really more interested in being saved from hell than in worshiping God.

Reared in a Polish Catholic family where the parish you belonged to was part of your family's identity, it would be un-thinkable for my parents to not send their children to a Catholic school.

My parents were humble believers. They obeyed the direction given them by the church and earnestly prayed to God each and every day. They taught us kids by their example, not so much by book lessons or Bible reading. They relied on our parochial school to teach us about the things of God.

Chapter 10: Hey God

As a kid, I lit candles and recited prayers like the "Our Father," the "Apostle's Creed" and "Hail Mary". These prayers meant nothing to me because I had no real connection with God; I only knew there was a God. I mimicked what I was taught and really made no decisions of my own on faith. I was baptized as a baby, which was my parents' decision. I received First Communion in the second grade because that's what I was told was supposed to happen. I received Holy Confirmation in the sixth grade, again because that was what was required of me.

Faith for me was on auto-pilot. I simply performed the designated obligations in conjunction with the designated schedule regardless of the fact that I held to no belief of my own. I had no idea there was such a thing as a relationship with God. That was no one's fault; I was just too immature to understand the human problem of sin. Religion for me was like earning Boy Scout badges. Most boys throw away their scout vests when they grow up.

My progression of faith really began after the birth of Janene. My desire to protect her led to my recognition of the need for salvation through Jesus Christ. With that came real prayers that engendered adoration. Those were humble prayers that stemmed from my heartfelt thankfulness because of what God had done for me. Bible study became a way of life and a change took place in me. I began to feel uncomfortable in my old environment.

I grew like spring grass, thick and healthy. I felt God was waiting for me each morning to wake up so He could treat me to a new experience. God's presence seemed to be evident everywhere I looked. Conversation with God was uncomplicated. Life had purpose, fulfillment, and joy. I praised God every day. Words jumped off the pages of the Bible as I read through it and the stories were stamped into my memory. I didn't have to make time to pray; I just did it, and enjoyed it. Those secure feelings of knowing I was on the same page as God were almost too hard to contain. Like hanging out with a favorite uncle who was always willing to buy you an ice-cream bar or take you for a ride in his car, God and I just seemed to click. Life was good, eternity absolute, and I felt special.

I got used to that feeling. After some years it just lost its newness and I took it for granted. That green-spring-grass feeling slowly turned summer brown. Somewhere along the way the adoration and appreciation diminished. My prayer list became more a wish list. My dialogue with God turned into a one-sided conversation that focused on my wants. Praying only about the things that mattered to me, I couldn't remember the last time I considered what might be important to God.

After the accident, even those weak one-sided conversations became fewer and fewer. Prayer became tedious. I longed for the days of conversational prayer that included praise and honesty but couldn't concentrate long enough to complete one prayer. So instead of closing my eyes and starting off with a prayer that was bound to segue into me thinking about how my shoes needed polishing or what I felt like for dinner, as prayer tended to turn out for me, I started reading the Book of James.

In the earlier years of my newfound faith I made great boasts and claimed to have all the right answers. In the wake of the accident my once-vital faith fell dormant. The Book of James is one of those get-your-attention books that offer realistic advice for believers who feel their faith is dead. James doesn't hem-haw; he confronts apathy and exposes hypocritical practices.

Immediately he hit me with:

> *"Consider it pure joy, my brothers and sisters, whenever you face trials of many kinds, because you know that the testing of your faith produces perseverance. Let perseverance finish its work so that you may be mature and complete, not lacking anything."*
>
> *~James 1:2-4*

"Mature"—that word really struck me. I never thought of myself as being immature.

> *"But someone will say, 'You have faith; I have deeds.' Show me your faith without deeds, and I will show you my faith by my deeds. You believe that there is one God.*

Back to Tonic

Good! Even the demons believe that—and shudder."
~James 2:18-19

When the book challenged me to show my faith by my deeds I couldn't point to any sincere service. I had returned to my childhood concept of God—*"only knowing of him."* Even worse, I wasn't shuddering.

At that, I simply started talking to God. Expressing my awareness of the obvious distance between us, I asked that He come toward me, meeting me halfway. While still blaming Him for His inaction I was willing to give Him a chance to explain so that we could repair the rift between us and return to our previous relationship. I was hoping for some kind of sign confirming that God actually acknowledged my prayer, but really didn't expect to get one.

After days of repeating that same dialogue before what seemed to be a closed door, I was moved to sit down at my keyboard. Call it an answer from God or whatever you want. I began to type these words:

> *"I didn't distance myself from you. I have been here all along. You chose to try to manage this thing that you have no control over. You don't understand it and it hurts. Your dreams have been shattered and you see no evidence of any kind of meaningful good coming from it. I understand. You don't think that I know*

how it feels. I do. I know how much it hurts. What you experienced was the pain of losing someone that you loved more than anything else. The price of love is grief. You loved Jacob so much that losing him affected you like nothing else ever has.

What I want is for you to love me as much as you loved Jacob. I want you to love me whole-heartedly. I want you to be willing to do for me the things that I ask out of love for me, just as you would have done for Jacob, without thinking twice about it. I want you to want to serve me. Your problem is that you don't want to. You feel you should, but you don't want to. You don't want to because your love for me is different than your love was for Jacob. You say you love me and you do, but I want to be the center of your life. Come close to me."[2]

After reading this I recalled what a friend had once said about his new wife and her boys. He hoped she could love him as much as she loved those boys. I would almost certainly give my life for my family, but I really doubt I would do the same for God. I loved God about as much as I could, but not as much as Jacob or the rest of my family.

---

2   I had an English professor take a look at the book when I first completed it. When she sent back the file it was full of track changes. Red notes filled every paragraph; except for the section above for the answer from God. It was flawless.

I had come to discover that I really didn't like God as much as I liked myself. When I asked God for help it was to help me accomplish what I wanted—for me. That's the real truth.

Church growth expert Win Arn went out and interviewed about 10,000 members of all kinds of congregations in America—nearly 1,000 churches. He asked, *"What is the purpose of your church?"* When he came back, he tabulated the results. Eighty-nine percent of the members said, *"The purpose of the church is to take care of me, my family and the other members."* Eleven percent of the typical church members said, *"The purpose of the church is to fulfill the Great Commission to win the world to Christ."*[19]

An honest portrayal of my thoughts on the church's purpose would place me in that eighty-nine percent bracket. I had fallen victim to a comfortable version of Christianity that stemmed from my selfishly creating an image of a God who was relevant in my world. Much like choosing options when buying a new car, I selected what I wanted in God and passed on what I didn't.

Who was the bigger fool, the person who attended church twice a year on Christmas and Easter believing that was all God required of him, or me who daily revered the idea of a God who approved of my self-centeredness?

Basically, everything I owned paid tribute to me. I had spent many hours working and sacrificing to acquire possessions that did little or nothing to promote the God I claimed to be at the center of my existence. I placed constraints on the amount of influence God had in my life and limited Him to being nothing more than a domestic worker whose main function was to satisfy my desires. Conveniently, I tossed the blame His way when my plans didn't work out.

If my life had been viewed from a position high above in the gondola of a hot air balloon I may have appeared to be a fairly devoted Christian. I attended worship services regularly and belonged to small group studies. I tithed to the church when I could and adopted a Bible reading plan. My children attended Sunday school classes and other youth activities. I even performed some community volunteer work. But landing the balloon and walking the streets would have revealed something different. The cracks that ran through my commitment could be seen at street level.

For the most part, God had just become ordinary to me, another social contact or prescription drug in the medicine cabinet to be used "as needed." Relying on my own ability to solve problems, I found little reason to genuinely give thanks to God or offer praise to Him. I just continued on with that part-time relationship believing that was the life God had intended me to live. Even worse, I thought the rest of the world would be better off if they imitated Christians like me.

I suppose that attitude is the byproduct of American Christianity where God often is used to promote our personal choices and our political views. We search for signs from God, or some *"God-thing"* sensation, that endorses our belief that God not only approves of our choices, but has willed them. We spend a lot of time trying to create heaven here on earth. I am pretty sure God promised heaven in heaven. Satan is the one who promotes the idea of heaven on earth.

Closer scrutiny brought my true sense of allegiance into view. My faith was at risk of becoming a collection of *"feel good"* ideas that inspired me to live what I believed to be a good life while ignoring some pretty specific instructions.

> *"'Love the Lord your God with all your heart and with all your soul and with all your mind.' This is the first and greatest commandment. And the second is like it: 'Love your neighbor as yourself.'"*
> ~ *Matthew 22:37-39*

How could I love God with *"all"* my heart, soul and mind if I changed His commandments to fit my preferences? Unfortunately, the ever-expanding mindsets of today's world tempt us to be centered on feel-good philosophies which on the surface appear focused on love; but love for whom?

Society seems to believe it has to take the wheel of the universe from the hands of God because His Bible no longer reflects what is true or actual in the world today. It prefers the open-minded view that Jesus came only to teach us to love. The Bible actually states His purpose as having come to "seek and save the lost." Not appreciating being labeled as lost, today's culture charges God with being out of touch and attempts to dictate tolerance by modifying His commandment from *"Love your neighbor"* into *"Accept sin and treat it as normal."*

If decisions on right and wrong were left to our own discretions, we could eliminate the complications of being labeled as *"lost"* and the uncomfortable notion of having to face God's judgment.

I don't think Jesus Christ would have suffered through the crucifixion and rose from the dead to teach us to become open-minded and ignore sin. He could have just simply stated that—we would have been happy to take on that principle.

Were my achievements and possessions what God intended for me?

The Rich Man and the Kingdom of God
"A certain ruler asked him, 'Good teacher, what must I do to inherit eternal life?' 'Why do you call me good?' Jesus answered. 'No one is good—except God alone. You know the commandments: "You shall not commit adultery, you shall not murder, you shall not steal, you shall not give false testimony, honor your father and mother."' 'All these I have kept since I was a boy,' he said. When Jesus heard this, he said to him, 'You still lack one thing. Sell everything you have and give to the poor, and you will have treasure in heaven. Then come,

follow me.' When he heard this, he became very sad,
because he was very wealthy. Jesus looked at him and
said, 'How hard it is for the rich to enter the kingdom
of God! Indeed, it is easier for a camel to go through the
eye of a needle than for someone who is rich to enter
the kingdom of God.' Those who heard this asked, 'Who
then can be saved?' Jesus replied, 'What is impossible
with man is possible with God.' Peter said to him, 'We
have left all we had to follow you!' 'Truly I tell you,'
Jesus said to them, 'no one who has left home or wife or
brothers or sisters or parents or children for the sake of
the kingdom of God will fail to receive many times as
much in this age, and in the age to come eternal life.'''

~ Luke 18:18-29

Narrowed down to its simplest form, the Bible seems absolutely clear about our purpose. God's followers are to worship Him, rely on Him, and spread His gospel to the lost. I was supposed to impact the world, but instead, I was worshiping the gods of nice neighborhoods, money, safety, education, stature, secure retirement, and everything else the world deems to be sensible or successful. Sadly, this is what many of us teach our children and we reproduce more Christians just like ourselves.

I did put Jacob and most everything else in my life before God. I wasn't well-off by any means, but I was living a relatively content life. I'm afraid as I strived for the American Dream God's place in my life became that of a personal assistant who had been given the task of fulfilling my dreams. I praised God when those dreams were on track, but when they got derailed I felt like he cheated me.

Years after losing Jake, while visiting Haiti, I found the people there in a better position to keep God at the center of their lives than most people I had known. The Haitians had relatively nothing in the way of possessions, but they appeared joyful. Because they had nothing, there was nothing to get in the way of them making God their top priority. On the contrary, most everything in my life got in the way of God.

Discovering the authentic God can be compared to my realizing that learning to swim would have been a good idea before I fell out of the boat. My comfortable image of God did not sustain me when my life was suddenly shattered.

While I had been a believer for 16 years before the accident, I guess I really wasn't all that mature. I was aware of God and what He had done for me, but didn't pay much attention to what He expected from me. I was untested and surely wasn't ready for what God would allow me to experience. People like to say God won't allow you to bear more than you can handle. Actually, that's not what the Bible says. The verse they refer to is about temptation, not troubles.

"No temptation has seized you except what is common to man. And God is faithful; He will not let you be tempted beyond what you can bear. But when you are

tempted, He will also provide a way out so that you can
stand up under it."

~I Corinthians 10:13

Instead, the Bible clearly states we may find ourselves "under great pressure, far beyond our ability to endure."

"We do not want you to be uninformed, brothers
and sisters, about the troubles we experienced in the
province of Asia. We were under great pressure, far
beyond our ability to endure, so that we despaired of
life itself. Indeed, we felt we had received the sentence
of death. But this happened that we might not rely on
ourselves but on God, who raises the dead."

~ 2 Corinthians 1:8-9

Could Jake's death have been the result of some lesson God had for me? The idea of Him using an accident like this as a *"lesson"* sounds pretty callous. If it wasn't a lesson, then why didn't He step in and stop it? Why didn't He act? Could God be some kind of cold, big-picture guy who is all about his will regardless of how that impacts people like me? I preferred my version of the personal God who watched out for me while I did the things that made me happy.

Jake the Puzzle Solver

Jake learned to play chess in the seventh grade. Within that one school year he rose to the top of the chess team, defeating

Chapter 10: Hey God

the esteemed and championship-winning math coach, Mr. DeVore. Jake went on that same year to take seventh place in the state competition.

He could figure out just about any shape logic puzzle. His first-grade teacher told us she had to buy harder puzzles because he solved the ones she had too quickly. Once in just ten minutes he solved a puzzle my dad and my brother Stanley had labored over for hours. I was in awe of Jake's intelligence and ability to quickly sort out most any enigma. Jake had what I lacked—clear and focused vision.

God had become my enigma, the puzzle that left me scratching my head and staring at the pieces. Maybe if Jacob had been here still he could have shown me how to make sense of those pieces. I could no longer think of God in terms of what I'd like Him to be. So that left me with the frightening aspect of knowing Him as He really is.

Some people say they can actually hear God's audible voice answering their prayers. I never have and don't really believe they have either. In fact, I don't know that I wanted to hear His voice. He may have sounded like Truman Capote and that would really have blown whatever image of Him I had left.

So who is God? Maybe the first question should be who am I?

Chapter 11

Who Am I

"It is the individual who knows how little they know about themselves who stands the most reasonable chance of finding out something about themselves before they die."[20]

~ S.I. Hayakawa

I have a love/hate relationship with the St. Louis Cardinals. I admire them as a team. They have been—and still are—arguably the best team in the National League. They seem to acquire the best managers, have loyal fans, and wear the best-looking uniforms in all of baseball. I, however, am a Cubs fan, and it is hard to heap too much praise on our greatest rival. Defeating the Cardinals is much more than just winning a baseball game. It is the pinnacle of happiness.

The Sandberg Game

Saturday, June 23, 1984, six-year-old Jacob became Ryne (Ryno) Sandberg's biggest fan. Jake and I were watching the Cubs/Cardinals game and our beloved Cubs were losing seven to one early in the game. Sandburg knocked in one run in the fifth inning, making it a seven to three game, but the Cardinals answered with two in the sixth, making it nine to three. The Cubs came back with five in the bottom of the sixth, two of which had been driven in by Sandburg's single. This game was getting exciting. Hope was in the air. Jacob went and got his mitt, smacking his fist into the glove as he jumped with excitement or collapsed with disappointment at each turn of events. Jake kept asking, *"When is Ryno up again?"*

With the Cardinals on top by a score of nine to eight and the great Bruce Sutter on the mound, it looked bleak. Jake rose to his feet as, leading off the ninth, Sandberg stepped up to the plate. Incredibly, Sandburg launched a game-tying homerun, and Jake leapt as we high-fived each other.

Chapter 11: Who Am I

The celebration was short-lived, though, as the Cardinals took a two-run lead in the tenth. Jake looked like a deflating balloon. With the Cubs down by a pair in the bottom of the tenth, Bruce Sutter retired the first two batters, but walked Bobby Dernier. Jake's eyes lit up as Sandberg came to bat with another chance against Bruce Sutter.

On the third pitch, Sandberg launched his second homer of the day into the bleachers in left center that tied the game at eleven. The Cubs would go on to beat the Cardinals, and Jacob had found himself a hero. What a game!

I guess we all could use a hero; someone who steps up and snatches victory from the jaws of defeat; someone who makes everything right. In my case that could only be God. Only God could right this wrong.

I had made a lot of mistakes in my life, but one thing is for sure: mistakes have helped mold me into the person I've become. My life's experiences have either helped to prepare me for this moment or hindered me in it.

It was time for me to stop being disappointed with God and people. It was time to start examining the heart of my disappointment. Had I been living with notions about myself that were just as mistaken as the ones I had about God?

My Christian journey began when I recognized Jesus Christ as my savior. I thought I was budding in my faith and began to see myself differently; but apparently not accurately. Improvement in my personal character seemed to be emerging. Maybe along with that improvement came some arrogance as well. I was thinking that the changes taking place in me were examples of what God does in the heart of a believer. I guess the hitch was that my heart hadn't changed nearly as much as my opinion of myself had.

I remember the day—no, I remember the actual moment— when I discovered a horrible truth about myself. I thought I had come to see all people as equal and was able to feel affection for people in the way Jesus asked us to. Then there was this breaking news release on television. It said there had been a house fire and three small children had been trapped inside. The fire department was unable to reach the children and all of them had died.

My heart broke as I thought about the anguish that family was about to go through and how empty their lives would be as a result of their tragic loss. I didn't just feel sympathy for this poor family on TV. Once again I relived the emotion of losing Jake.

In the next scene the mother of the children appeared on TV, and I felt my heart sighing with relief because she was black. The children were African American. I sat motionless as I realized what had just happened. I have no words to express how much that revelation utterly humbled me. If I could have gotten up and abandoned my body at that moment I would have.

There are haters aplenty in society today. No race is exempt from having people with superiority complexes. I just didn't think I was one of them. In the light of God, I was exposed for what I actually was. I saw the person God sees, and I was mortified. If left for me to do, my heart would never change. God was going to have to do some parenting with me.

"Tell me and I forget, teach me and I may remember, involve me and I learn."[21]

~ *Benjamin Franklin*

Raising children is a difficult and full-time job. Jan and I had three. They were all special in different ways. Our oldest, Janene, was the joy of our lives. She was the perfect little girl. She had big, beautiful, dark-brown eyes that just melted you when she gazed at you. She looked adorable and was extremely well-behaved. Janene really changed what Jan and I considered important. Overnight, she became the center of our universe, and we changed from married kids to aspiring responsible parents.

As is common with a lot of children, Janene became a little difficult when she entered her teen years. She started to rebel and, as that rebellion continued, we realized we had to start withholding some of her privileges. She complained that we loved Jacob more because he always got to do whatever he wanted.

Truth was, Jacob was a special boy. He not only obeyed, but for the most part, he obeyed gladly. When he asked for something within reason we many times granted his requests because of his obedience. Janene, on the other hand, was denied many things. We wanted to give her all we could, but we just couldn't allow her to think it was okay for her to go on acting the way she did and still reaping rewards. We had high hopes for her.

She said she hated us and accused us of never loving her. How could she say that? She was my pride and joy. She was a part of me. I lay awake at night trying to figure out how I could protect her from the dangers of the world. She was the cause of me finding my salvation.

After the accident, Janene had some of her own anger to deal with. She started hanging around with some people we felt were bad influences. One night as I was getting ready to leave for a special function she told me she was going out with these people. I said she couldn't, and an argument started. She said she'd leave as soon as I left, so I stayed home. Not to be defeated, she told me she'd leave as soon as I went to bed and I couldn't stop her. So I took a chair from the kitchen, set it in front of her bedroom door and sat there—all night. I couldn't allow her to risk destroying her life by getting involved in something harmful. I had to stop her.

Chapter 11: Who Am I

Wasn't my attitude toward God exactly like Janene's had been toward me? I was questioning whether or not God loved me. Life after the accident wasn't all that great. I watched others getting stuff while all I got was heartache. Where was my stuff? I remember telling God I didn't think He loved me. That's when my words to Janene rang in my ear: *"How could I love anyone more?"*

That hit me like a brick. How long had God been sitting outside my door preventing me from ruining my life? How long had I been claiming salvation without actually knowing the Savior? Did I come to Christ? Or did I merely choose the *"Christ option"* out of a long list of things to believe in? I had no clue of the danger I was setting myself up for.

> *"Not everyone who says to me, 'Lord, Lord,' will enter the kingdom of heaven, but only the one who does the will of my Father who is in heaven. Many will say to me on that day, 'Lord, Lord, did we not prophesy in your name and in your name drive out demons and in your name perform many miracles?' Then I will tell them plainly, 'I never knew you. Away from me, you evildoers!'*
> ~ *Matthew 7:21*

Now I was at the point where I could not distinguish between what I knew and what I believed. I wondered if I had just been going through the motions for the past 16 years. My *"motions"* were about to be tested as I was fortunate enough to have the unfortunate experience of capsizing a canoe on a flooded river.

The River

I clung to the log for what seemed like more than half an hour. The cold water poured over my head and my legs and right arm felt numb. I was clutching something with my left hand and didn't recall taking hold of anything. Turning my wrist as much as I could and straining to see over the slimy log, I caught a glimpse of what I chose to save from the river's current; it was a box of my homemade fishing spinners. It's odd what possessions we find important enough to hold onto. There I was, just me and my spinners, clinging to a slippery log as night fell on a cold flooded river.

It was a typically cold and gray afternoon in early spring along the Kankakee River. My lifelong friend Bill and I had decided to fish the backwater area on the Indiana side in spite of the fact that the river was at flood stage. We launched my canoe east of Momence, Illinois, and planned to skirt up-river and under the State Line Bridge. We would then move off into the backwater area.

It was a dumb idea, but dumb ideas were nothing new to us. Friends since the age of nine, Bill and I often found ourselves in some predicament because of our inability to think things through before proceeding. Once he shot me in the left hand

Chapter 11: Who Am I

with a 22-caliber pistol as we argued whose turn it was with the gun. He shot himself with a bow and arrow, which in itself is quite an accomplishment. And the coup de grâce was when he shot himself through the groin with a 357 magnum pistol while attempting to take the gun apart. Yeah, together we were an accident waiting to happen.

The Kankakee River was so high that in order to pass beneath State Line Bridge we had to lie on our backs and use our hands to pull the canoe under. We made it through and continued up-river to a backwater area where we fished for several hours. Unlike the river, the backwater was still. We saw one other boat that came in from up-river to avoid the peril of maneuvering under the bridge.

Bill hooked a seven-pound northern pike. Naturally, we had left the landing net back in the car. I told him to bring the fish to the side of the canoe and I would grab it by hand. As the pike swam alongside the boat, I quickly caught it behind the head with my right hand and yanked it out of the water, just like on TV.

Oh, we were just so impressed with ourselves and our outdoor abilities. We laughed at the guys in the other boat who had a thermometer and were checking the water temperature. Outdoorsmen like us wouldn't waste our time with instrumentation.

Fishing was slow and nightfall was approaching. We decided to head back to the car. Traveling down-river was a different story. The current was strong and pushed us along at a very fast pace. The bridge came on us like a speeding truck and Bill couldn't lie back quickly enough to clear the bridge beam. He hit the bridge. The force of the water behind us turned the canoe sideways. That threw me into the side of the bridge beam and the boat flipped, dumping us into the cold water.

We grabbed onto the canoe and drifted with it. I never considered life preserver cushions to be anything more than a requirement of the law. After all, only an idiot would fall out of a boat and need one. Now they seemed like a good thing to be in possession of. Both the cushions floated down to my end, so I let go of the boat in order to capture them before they slipped away. I tossed one over to Bill, but the canoe had drifted out of my reach. All I had to cling to was the seat cushion. Bill and the canoe floated toward the north channel and I was drawn into the main channel.

That area is famous for a major logjam that had actually changed the flow of the river back in the early nineteen-hundreds. The main river now turned south, but the old north channel still flowed up to the old logjam and then tunneled underneath. The undertow is powerful and many people have drowned there over the years.

I attempted to swim toward the shore, but not wanting to let go of the life preserver made progress slow and difficult.

Chapter 11: Who Am I

Realizing I was at risk of being pulled into the dangerous north channel, I decided to swim back toward the main stream and take my chances there. I knew there were sand bars in the main channel that shallowed the river's depth and I hoped to utilize one of them to make my escape.

As I approached the peninsula that split the main river from the north channel, I spotted a lesser log jam jutting out from the front edge. It lay directly in my path and I was rapidly approaching. The current hurled me into the logs. Fortunately, the seat cushion softened the blow to my chest. As my body was thrown under the jam I caught my left armpit on the leading log. The flow rushed over my head, pushing hard and forcing me further under the jam.

It was mid-April and the water was frigid. I didn't know what had happened to Bill. I began to assess my situation. It was nearly dark and things didn't look good. If I let go of the log I'd be swept under the jam. There was no guarantee I would find an opening near the front of the peninsula where I could climb out. I might find myself trapped beneath the log jam and drown. My body was parallel to the underside of the jam and the water was moving with such force that I couldn't pull my right arm up to gain a better grip on the log. It felt similar to the force you feel holding your arm out a car window at eighty miles an hour.

Attempts to pull my right arm out from the undertow weakened my anchored left arm's grip on the slippery log. I didn't have the strength to pull myself up with just one arm. It was becoming pretty clear that the only way to get out of this predicament was to have someone rescue me, and there was no one around.

I was shivering. As minutes passed, I recognized my situation was hopeless. We were in the middle of nowhere. I presumed that Bill had drowned in the north channel and I would be joining him shortly. I could feel myself weakening and knew it would be just a matter of time before I would lose hold and slip under the logs.

Cold and on my own in what had turned into a pitch dark night, I let the box of spinners go. They no longer seemed important. The sound of water rushing over my head became a sort of rhythmic melody of death almost like an organ softly playing in the background as the people entered the church for my funeral.

I thought of my family. How could I do this to them? How could I be so irresponsible? I was angry with myself—and then it occurred to me—I wasn't scared. I wasn't afraid to die. Although I had been questioning my faith, I did seem to have it. My faith was real.

I really didn't know what to expect next, but I anticipated something good awaited me on the other side. I hung beneath that log jam waiting on my dying breath when faintly, over the sound of the rushing water, I could hear distant voices. As the voices drew nearer I noticed waves of oscillating light reflecting off the outstretched arms of the peninsula's treetops. I expected to see angels come bursting out of the night sky at any moment. I was ready.

The angels turned out to be two guys in a fishing boat. Someone driving over the bridge had witnessed us capsizing and had located a nearby game warden. The warden commandeered two fishermen from further downstream and they bravely came to my aide. The river current slammed their boat into the logs, pinning me between. It took several attempts to finally pull me away from my peril. One man held onto me as I clung to the gunwale while the helmsman slowly fought the current back to the river bank.

Bill was already on shore. The canoe had pushed him close enough that he had managed to grab hold of an exposed tree root and pull himself onto the bank. The great outdoorsmen had survived yet another near-disaster.

After an hour warming ourselves at a fire and regaining the feeling in our limbs, the warden let us leave. He told us when people fall into this area of the river at flood stage he expects to find bodies, not survivors.

Leaving there, I realized I was at least in possession of a faith in God's eternal promise, weak and wavering as it might be.

Trusting God with things here on earth, on the other hand, was something I was going to have to work on. Something needed to change, and I had the feeling God wasn't about to move away from His view of things.

Since I arrived home much later than expected, Jan already knew something had gone wrong. As her facial expression of relief and gratitude turned to anger, she informed me I wouldn't be *"playing"* with Bill again anytime soon.

Faith

In my opinion, there seems to be three main steps to a proper relationship with God: faith, trust and submission. Faith is the confidence or belief in something when there is no material proof. It's that step between promise and assurance that prompts us to seek God. I undeniably believed in God without a need to physically prove He existed. Apparently, faith isn't something we discover on our own, but we each come equipped with a certain measure of it.

> " ... *God has allotted to each a measure of faith.*"
> ~ *Romans 12:3*

It's sort of like a faith starter kit. God has rooted a certain amount of faith in the consciences of all people and it kind of runs there on auto-pilot. It's where the instinct we have concerning right and wrong and the feeling of guilt come from. It's where the call to inquire about God originates.

Chapter 11: Who Am I

I have often ignored my conscience, but never won an argument with it.

Faith is like a tattoo; you can cover it up but it won't wash off. A strong faith is the product of exercising it.

Trust

Trust is a different issue. According to Wikipedia, trust is the reliance on another person or entity. I had relied on God, and from my perspective, He had failed me. Salvaging that trust wasn't going to be easy, especially being that I would never hear God's side of the story. I was just left to guess what He may or may not have been thinking. It was a huge stumbling block in my effort to move forward spiritually. Unfortunately I wasn't equipped with a default button that when pressed would reset our relationship. It wasn't that easy.

It's said that trust is earned. How then would God earn my trust? Was that a legitimate question? Trust Him to do what? The Bible states numerous and often conflicting ways in which God interacts with people. I needed to know what to expect if I was to trust it would happen. Clarity isn't found in open-ended assurances that God should be trusted to look out for my best interests. I may have found it easier to trust Him if I could have identified some tangible intervention from my past.

Gideon said to God,
*"...I will place a wool fleece on the threshing floor. If
there is dew only on the fleece and all the ground is dry,
then I will know that you will save Israel by my hand, as
you said." And that is what happened. Gideon rose early
the next day; he squeezed the fleece and wrung out the
dew—a bowlful of water.*

Then Gideon said to God,
*"Do not be angry with me. Let me make just one more
request. Allow me one more test with the fleece. This
time make the fleece dry and the ground covered with
dew."*

~ Judges 6:36-40

Then again, how many signs would it have taken before
my indecisive, wavering faith would have been able to trust
without question?

Submission

Submission is probably the toughest of the three, especially
without complete trust. Submission requires more than an
intellectual response, more than just agreeing with God.
Submission means taking the final say away from me and
giving it to God. I hadn't done that—ever! I didn't know if I
could.

I was facing an enormous crisis of faith. I had collided with
a Titanic-sized iceberg of reality and my long-avowed views

had been taking on water. I couldn't deny the supremacy of God and I hated the idea of having to start over again, but this relationship required more than just a patch job.

It's a fortunate man that recognizes the mistakes he's made before it's too late to correct them. It's a humbled man that actually sets out to correct them. I had much to reflect on, and it felt as if I had been trying to take a drink from an open fire hydrant. The rush of thoughts was overwhelming.

PART III

"The Turnaround

Chapter 12

My Personal Jesus

"I believe in the sun even when it's not shining, and in love, even when I'm alone, and in God, even when He is silent."[22]

(Found scratched into a wall at a Nazi Concentration Camp)

Back to Tonic

It was in the forty-eighth year of my life that I was finally ready to see myself as being accountable for much of my misery. It wasn't just the accident. I had been on-guard all my life, unwilling to give over to emotion or failure. The accident and what happened over the following eight years pushed me back against the wall, and the only way out was forward.

The largest obstacle in accomplishing that movement was me. Facing me was nearly as hard as facing God, but I needed to contend with myself before I could honestly approach Him. I was still far from admitting I was wrong. I needed to find a warm place of safety in which to hole up and begin to process my thoughts.

As a young boy my warm safe spot was the little house we called home. My mom and dad worked hard, sacrificed often, and provided us with a good life. One thing I knew for sure was that I was loved in that home. I could return there and find comfort no matter what I had done. My troubles seemed to lessen when I spotted the welcoming lamplight shining from our little home. I knew love was waiting there for me.

The accident was responsible for more than Jake's death. It also caused me to see how irrational my beliefs had become. I gave little thought to the notion that the divine being who created heaven and earth would also insist on absolute authority over it. This wasn't the warm and fuzzy God I had gotten used to. He was a powerful monarch who held the final word on everything.

Chapter 12: My Personal Jesus

Much like the comforting sight of that little warm home, I thought that if I could find my way back to the presence of the loving God I once knew things might get better. Preventing me from doing so was the notion that He wouldn't recognize me as I now was, and I had become just another face in the crowd.

> "Some men came carrying a paralyzed man on a mat and tried to take him into the house to lay him before Jesus. When they could not find a way to do this because of the crowd, they went up on the roof and lowered him on his mat through the tiles into the middle of the crowd, right in front of Jesus."
>
> ~ Luke 5:18-19

Afraid to approach God on my own, I was hoping someone would approach Him for me. I was searching for my own personal Ryno who, when all hope was gone, would step up to the plate and knock it out of the park, saving me from the jaws of defeat. I never found my Ryno. It was just as well; even Ryne Sandberg struck out—1260 times, to be exact.

Isolation seemed to be my safest haven. I didn't feel safe exposing such deep turmoil to just anybody. Backing away from people was easier, especially church people whom I believed continued to look for me to be a strong example of faith. My defense became not allowing anyone to get too close. That way I didn't have to worry about being disappointed, or disappointing anyone else.

Back to Tonic

The nightmares and visions continued. They were probably the result of having no outlet for my struggles. Jan surmised that my mind needed to release this inner turmoil, so it let loose some of the mayhem in my sleep when I wasn't in control, or in a moment of deep sorrow. She called it a natural release, not a man going insane. Still, something didn't seem right. God should have protected me from the anxiety and horror.

I was aware of what God had promised his followers. The surfacing question became whether or not I was excluded from that group. Could it have been that my name wasn't listed in the *"Book of Life"* along with those destined for heaven as Paul mentions in Philippians 4:3? Theologian John Calvin interpreted biblical predestination to mean that God willed eternal damnation for some people and salvation for others. Could salvation really only be available to those God wanted, and I wasn't wanted?

I could see that I didn't demonstrate affection for God in the same manner as others I'd seen in church. I didn't raise my hands in the air and wave them about or go into long tear-filled public prayers. Those actions seemed to reflect a relationship with God much deeper than mine. But my expression of love for God was very characteristic of how I expressed love in all my other relationships.

If God was going to predetermine who He wanted and who He didn't, why not just create the winners, and let them go directly to eternal paradise? Why bother to create the losers? And if everything is pre-determined, what is the definition of free will? The Bible appears to describe people as authors of their own deeds and deciders of their own fates. In Deuteronomy, the Israelites were given a choice:

"This day I call the heavens and the earth as witnesses against you that I have set before you life and death, blessings and curses. Now choose life, so that you and your children may live"

~ Deuteronomy 30:19

Saint Francis was once so convinced he was going to hell that he stayed in bed agonizing for several weeks. Then one day he got up and decided if he couldn't spend eternity loving God he could at least love Him right now.

Would there be an advantage to having God in your life now if you knew He wouldn't be in your future? Would God even acknowledge a prayer from someone He had already predestined for hell? Would prayer be worth the trouble?

There sure are a lot of people around who seem to be living like they're headed for hell. Seemingly conscienceless people who commit heinous crimes appear to have already reserved a place in eternal hell. I wondered, would I lead a different life if I knew heaven was not an option for me? Who would be willing to give up their earthly possessions to follow Jesus with no guarantee of a heavenly reward? I'm afraid I was becoming much like the rich man who asked what it would take to follow Jesus. I wanted some clearly outlined assurances before I would take any risks.

Some people say things happen for a reason. They seek some kind of instant rationalization that will serve to explain the unexplainable and bring harmony back to their souls. I don't believe everything has been predestined. Could it be most of the time things happen just because they happen? God Almighty unquestionably has the power to do as He wishes, but for the most part maybe He just lets the consequences of the free will He gave us govern. The words *"God's Will"* and *"God's Control"* cannot be properly defined in Webster's Dictionary. God's definition of *"control"* is obviously different than mine. God may not like the consequences of my free-will decisions, but I'll bet with a little cooperation on my part He can use them to make me stronger; maybe even incorporate them into whatever it is He's doing. After all, He is the *"Great Adjuster."*

In my search for clarity, I've found that many people are unclear on faith, the Bible, and what to expect in this life. Not everyone is as absolutely confident as they first appear. But those who are possess a genuine Christian hope. It's an entirely different concept from the therapeutic process of positive thinking used to reverse doubt. This hope is the real anticipation of obtainment.

Chapter 12: My Personal Jesus

Dr. Barbara L. Fredrickson, Principal Investigator of the Positive Emotions and Psychophysiology Lab and Professor at the University of North Carolina, Chapel Hill, argues that hope "...comes into play when our circumstances are dire," [23]

That kind of hope longs for the winning lottery ticket to reverse their bad luck. Christian hope is in play always, in both good times and bad.

"For in this hope we were saved. But hope that is seen is no hope at all. Who hopes for what they already have?"
~ *Romans 8:24*

My personal obstacle in holding fast to the hope I had in Christ Jesus was that He also allowed me to be hurt so badly through the loss of Jacob. I felt somewhat like the submissive partner in an abusive relationship—expected to obey without question with no say in the matter. It was a struggle I didn't want to be caught up in.

I believe the "Average Joe" struggles with more spiritual issues than he'd like to admit. Some people are aggressive and feel the need to prove everything they believe. It has to make sense to them or they won't sit still until it does. Some people are very passive and just refuse to press to resolve any questions or doubts they have. They smile, say things like, "Everything happens for a reason," and hope nobody asks them to explain that adaptive reasoning. Some are just apathetic, latching onto a partial view that's comfortable and leaving it at that; out of sight, out of mind.

Faith is ripened through the spiritual environment we choose to inhabit. It's the result of a tested education. Trust is just a word until the time comes when we are forced to use it. Adoration doesn't mean quite as much until the time comes when we bow and adore the One we blame for allowing us to hurt. The act of sacrifice means nothing to us if we are unaware of its heavy cost. Can we really identify with meaningful giving if we have never received support in our time of desperate need?

The Raven

Ravens are among the birds considered unclean by the Jews. According to Jewish tradition, the raven was the first bird Noah sent out from the ark to look for land. The raven never returned to the ark, instead roaming the earth on the floating carcasses of the flood victims. Jesus used this detestable bird as a measure of comparison in regard to how He valued his disciples.

> *"Then Jesus said to his disciples: 'Therefore I tell you, do not worry about your life, what you will eat; or about your body, what you will wear. For life is more than food, and the body more than clothes. Consider the ravens: They do not sow or reap, they have no storeroom or barn; yet God feeds them. And how much more valuable you are than birds!'"*
>
> ~ Luke 12:22-24

Chapter 12: My Personal Jesus

There was a homeless man named Earl (my own personal raven) who begged at the stop light under the railway bridge near where I worked. Earl was truly homeless, carrying everything he owned with him because he had no place to store it. Some days he'd just lie on the side of the road with his shoes off and wave his cup. If he had been a woman with a small child people would probably have been more willing to reach out and help him. Unfortunately, he was nasty-looking and smelled awful, so most people just drove right past him.

I think God may have put Earl there just for me. He was at the opposite end of what is considered the American Dream. How he arrived at that low place in life really didn't matter; he was there. I knew he was desperate because he'd be waiting there in the freezing cold, the pouring rain and the summer heat. He didn't know what else to do. Earl was well past worrying about self-esteem. He was well past being humbled by his situation. He had a soft, weak voice and always thanked me when I gave him something; not a polite thank you showing good manners, but a relieved thank you given out of desperation. I clipped some money to the sun visor of my car so whenever I got stopped at the light I could give it to him. One time I handed him money attached to a pair of socks because his feet looked like they were killing him. I didn't give him something every day, but I did do it routinely.

Honestly, my generosity was not driven by obedience to Jesus' command to feed and clothe the poor. I wish I could say it was. I gave to him because I saw desperation in his eyes.

I believed Earl mattered to God, and if a lowly person like Earl mattered to Him, I must matter to Him as well.

Jacob noted something similar in his journal when he wrote he couldn't believe how desperately poor the people were who sat in the street outside the huge old Catholic church in Mexico City. Inside, the church was filled with opulence and gold relics, but outside it displayed lack of benevolence. Jake questioned how people could love God so much yet neglect to love people.

I don't know that I could honestly claim to love God if I didn't feel some measure of compassion for people like Earl. Yet love for God wasn't confirmed based on what filled my hand; He was probably more interested in what filled my heart. The majority of people passing by found it easier to judge Earl, shaking their heads in disgust and assuming he would just use any money he got for alcohol. A lot of those who demeaned Earl claimed to be church-going Christians.

It is estimated that roughly seventy-seven percent of people in American consider themselves to be Christians and around forty-four percent of those calling themselves Christians claim the biblical title of *"born again."*

"Jesus replied, 'Very truly I tell you, no one can see the kingdom of God unless they are born again.'"
~ John 3:3

Chapter 12: My Personal Jesus

I wonder how many of them have struggled like me. Do they really understand their faith or do they just check off the box labeled Christian on a questionnaire?

It's said that millions of children right here in America go to bed hungry each night. Has God been silent to their cries or have we been silent in our response? I wonder if God has been looking at those of us who should know better and asking, *"Why are children going to bed hungry?"* I doubt they'd use our support to buy alcohol.

I understood feeling isolated from a silent God and the church family I thought would have responded differently. I wanted to be strong again and acquire the level of faith of the person who had scratched those words on the concentration camp wall.

Faithful

Recently, a gunman opened fire at a small Christian university in California, killing seven people and wounding three more. In an interview, a student there said she wasn't afraid because she knew God would protect her.

While discussing this at work, a coworker asked why she felt God would protect her, but not the others. He asked, *"Weren't they all Christians?"* Another guy responded that she was spared because her faith was stronger. Strong faith spared her? Wouldn't that mean her faith was not only stronger than the other ten people shot at that school, but it was stronger than that of Jacob and the other boys, and stronger than the one million Christian martyrs in the first decade of the 21st Century?

> *"The International Bulletin of Missionary Research*
> *publishes an annual 'Status of Global Missions' report.*
> *The 2011 report involves martyrdom. The report defines*
> *'martyrs' as 'believers in Christ who have lost their*
> *lives, prematurely, in situations of witness, as a result*
> *of human hostility.' The report estimates that there*
> *were, on average, 270 new Christian martyrs every 24*
> *hours over the past decade, such that 'the number of*
> *martyrs [in the period 2000-2010] was approximately 1*
> *million.'"*[24]
>
> ~ *George Weigel*
> *Christian Number-Crunching, Feb 9, 2011*

There have been far too many faithful people who have suffered and died defending their faith to simply claim a strong faith will protect a person from harm.

I have come to believe that faith may more truly be measured in attitude. I met a man I consider to possess great faith, Dr. T Lunkim of the Kuki Christian Church, one of the largest Christian congregations in Northeast India. A few months after being released from 60 days of captivity, he was driving out to visit a mission site when he was met by a militant group blocking the road. One of the militants raised his gun to the car window. Dr. Lunkim looked the young man pointing the gun directly in the eyes and smiled. He said, *"I am not scared.*

Chapter 12: My Personal Jesus

If you kill me I will just go to heaven. If you let me live I will just have more time to help other people go to heaven. So whether you kill me or not, it is up to you. But I don't care and am not afraid." For me, faith just doesn't get much stronger than that.

Through history I've found that sometimes faithful people are blessed for the glory of God, and sometimes they suffer for it. As a result of Stephen's death in Acts 8:1-4, Christians were scattered and spread the message of salvation wherever they went. The church multiplied throughout Judea and Samaria. His death seemed to accomplish God's purposes.

"In their hearts humans plan their course, but the LORD establishes their steps."
~ Proverbs 16:9

I wonder how Jacob would feel knowing that his death led to the awakening of his father.

"Before you can draw, you have to learn to see."

Chapter 13

Where's MY Stuff?

"Ask and it will be given to you; seek and you will find; knock and the door will be opened to you."

~ Matthew 7:7

What's going wrong when we don't get what we ask for? Does God really answer prayers or not?

A whole lot of people say God answers prayer in one of three ways: yes, no, or wait. I guess I can understand that notion if we're talking about praying for a new home or car, but in matters of illness or life and death that view of prayer seems awfully insensitive.

The benefit in that perspective is that it helps us believe we actually received an answer. In reality, unless the answer is yes, we're left with no definitive answer at all.

If asked the question, *"Does God really answer my prayers?"* I would be more comfortable responding that I don't know. Does He even bother to consider the prayers that fall outside of His purposes? The Book of John, chapter nine, talks about Jesus healing a man who was born blind. In verse three, Jesus presents the reason for the man's blindness: *"But this happened so that the works of God might be displayed in him."* Think about that for a moment. God allowed that man's blindness from birth through adulthood so Jesus could heal him and demonstrate the power of God. God prearranged the man's blindness to advance His own purposes. That being the case, it would seem that the prayers which coincide with His will are more likely to be heard.

Chapter 13: Where's MY Stuff?

"We know that God does not listen to sinners. He listens to the godly person who does his will."

~ *John 9:31*

Some prayers would seem to fall within our vision of God's will, but just because it makes sense to us doesn't mean it's going to be willed by God. A very good friend of mine named Ron was dying of throat cancer. I went with three other guys to visit him in the hospital. His wife was in the room with him, and we had been talking for a while when one of the guys asked if we could all pray for Ron. That sounded like a great idea, so we gathered around him and one guy pulled a small bottle of oil out of his pocket to anoint Ron as we prayed. He proclaimed that because of Ron's strong faith, and because of God's goodness, Ron would be healed from this terrible illness. He said that God takes care of those He loves. God protects his followers and would restore Ron to health. Right after that we left the room.

That prayer really bothered me. When we got to the parking lot I asked the guy why he thought he could make promises for God. I said that Ron's wife was sitting right there listening to that prayer. What happens if Ron dies? What is she to think? According to his prayer, Ron's dying would mean he didn't have a strong faith or that God didn't love Ron because He didn't heal him.

The guy told me we need to be positive when we pray. I don't think that was being positive; that was putting words in God's mouth. I think making promises for God can only be viewed as arrogant or ignorant. In this case, I'm going with ignorant. Ron died soon after that. I never saw that guy again. I wonder if he is still as positive today about what God will and will not do in our lives.

When I pray for something significant and there appears to be no response God seems uncaring. I need to know my prayer was heard, that He gave my request some consideration. When nothing happens I can only try to believe that He reacted with one of the other two possible answers: no or wait. I have to believe that, because if He doesn't answer in one of those three ways, the only other possibilities left are either He doesn't listen to me, or He doesn't exist.

I find it difficult to accept lack of response as being an answer, especially when my request is for a pressing need. It appears to be more a failure to *"show up"* than it does an answer. It's hard for me to wrap my mind around the idea of a loving God who allows His loved ones to experience pain, sorrow and loss, especially if that suffering had been prearranged to fulfill God's own purposes.

Obviously I've been analyzing all this through human eyes and human desires. A better perspective of how to pray could possibly lead to a clearer understanding of the purpose of prayer. The Lord's Prayer in Matthew 6:9-13 is meant to be an outline of how to pray:

Chapter 13: Where's MY Stuff?

"Our Father, which art in heaven,
Hallowed be thy Name.
Thy Kingdom come.
Thy will be done in earth,
As it is in heaven.
Give us this day our daily bread.
And forgive us our trespasses,
As we forgive them that trespass against us.
And lead us not into temptation,
But deliver us from evil.
For Thine is the kingdom, the power, and the glory,
For ever and ever. Amen."

Nowhere do I see any part that focuses on my desires. I also don't see where God is asking my opinion or looking for advice. I see six steps: Worship, Surrender, Trust, Repentance, Seeking Deliverance, and Praise. The first two steps focus completely on God, and that's what I need to do—put God first. The next three focus on my response to God. And the last one brings me back to God.

One important step that applies to my situation is trust: *"Give us today our daily bread."* Daily bread for the Israelites in the wilderness was just enough manna to last one day. God provided them with food, water and guidance in the form of a cloud by day and fire by night. But people still got sick, and people still died. Death is actually an element of God's structure here on earth. It <u>will</u> happen. Death is also our reminder that this life is only temporary. God rationed the manna because his intention was to assist the Israelites as they passed though the wilderness and on to the Promised Land. He didn't want them getting comfortable where they were. Therefore, they came to rely on God's *"daily bread."*

Is *"daily bread"* different from *"good gifts"*? Does one reflect fundamental need while the other represents personal desires?

> *"If you, then, though you are evil, know how to give*
> *good gifts to your children, how much more will your*
> *Father in heaven give good gifts to those who ask Him!"*
> *~ Matthew 7:11*

If I, in fact, do matter to God, then it would stand to reason He would want to give me *"good gifts."* But who decides what a good gift is? I'll bet my idea of a *"good gift"* is drastically different than that of a starving Haitian child.

Had I gotten so comfortable in my own personal wilderness that I lost the desire to follow God out of it? My prayers had been centered on having Him join me there and giving little consideration to anything else.

NO

There are countless unwanted pregnancies each year, many of which are willfully terminated. I wonder how many of

Chapter 13: Where's MY Stuff?

those children would have brought the joy into someone's life that our daughter Cherie has brought to ours, and to many others as well.

I remember that when Jan and I thought she might be pregnant for the third time we were pretty upset. We didn't have the money or the room for another child. Jan and I talked about what we were going to do, and we decided to sincerely pray that the test would be negative, that God would not allow her to be pregnant. I remember saying, *"I just want two children."*

Today I have just two living children, Cherie being our third child. She is a teacher, a motivational speaker, and a missionary. She has an unbelievable thirst and love for God and love for others. Many people talk about compassion; Cherie demonstrates it. She is not defined by what she puts on display, but by who she is, every day. She's a contributor, not a consumer.

Her first mission trip to Kenya, Africa, was very hard on Jan, Janene and me. Watching her leave, knowing there was no guarantee she would be safe, weighed heavily on us. Praying to God to provide a safe return takes on a whole new dimension when you experienced a *"no"* to that prayer fifteen years earlier. It would have been easier to pray for the trip to be canceled.

I really couldn't claim I trusted her safety to God because I had trusted Him with Jake. I could only trust that God would accomplish in Cherie whatever it was He had planned for her, and pray that I would be able to accept that outcome. So we gathered at the church where her group was preparing to set off for Africa. We prayed together and said goodbye, but as that van drove away it was all I could do to keep from running after it.

Kenya was an awakening for Cherie. She observed a more pure and humble worship than we see here. She witnessed joy in the face of despair and thankfulness where there didn't appear to be anything to be thankful about. Unimaginable poverty compounded illnesses that here at home would have been easily treated. In Kenya those illnesses escalated into life-threatening conditions. The people there just seemed to accept their circumstances in life and went about living with what they had. Unlike Americans, they didn't appear to feel entitled; instead they just seemed content. Cherie went on to Haiti a few years later. She uses her experiences in motivational speaking and teaching.

I can't imagine life without Cherie, and I'm so grateful God ignored our foolish prayer to not allow that pregnancy. Our lives have been abundantly blessed through her life.

Yes

I can't imagine life without Jan either. One afternoon I returned home from work and found Jan sitting in her chair.

Chapter 13: Where's MY Stuff?

Something was up because she was supposed to be at work. She asked me to come and sit down. She told me she had received the results from some recent tests, and her doctor informed her she had uterine cancer. The biopsy was positive.

Just typing that makes me struggle to breathe. I just started sobbing. There is no other Jan! There's no one who could ever come close to loving me the way she does. She more than completes me; she is me. If she dies you might as well bury my heart along with her because it will never again be of any value to me. She has always been all I have ever wanted.

I remember when we were dating I would come home after an evening with her and I'd momentarily catch a whiff of her perfume on me. I would frantically keep sniffing so as not to lose her scent. I continued to taste her lips and recall the touch of her hand. She had a gentle and pure spirit about her, and I wondered what it was she saw in me. I never considered her as mine, but rather me as hers.

I just sat there, devastated. I don't know what is harder to absorb, learning someone I love was just killed as was the case with Jacob, or learning someone I love may have her life cut short. In both cases, I was powerless to do anything about it. Again I would have to go the God who answered "no" to Jake's safe return.

So how could I pray about this? After all, I'd been here before and the response wasn't what I'd hoped for. I prayed with Jan.

Back to Tonic

I prayed with my girls. I prayed with my friends. I prayed by myself. I prayed myself out. I asked Jan if she would mind having the elders at church gather around her and pray. She thought that was a good idea, so they laid hands on her and anointed her with oil as they prayed for a complete healing.

We went into Chicago to Rush University Medical Center and saw the top oncology/gynecologist in this area. The doctor said this particular type of cancer had the greatest success rate. He explained everything that needed to be done and the additional precautionary steps he would take to insure that all the cancer was removed.

We remained as positive as we possibly could. I would not allow myself to think about anything other than hearing the doctor say they were able to remove all the cancer and it hadn't spread.

The day of the surgery was similar to sitting in the airport waiting to fly out to Mexico, feeling like that man on death row. Jan was confident, and I was numb. I kissed her as she was rolled into the surgery waiting room. That kiss felt like a milestone. When she returned we would be looking at one of two things; we'd either be at the threshold of the end or at the beginning of the next part of our life together.

Some good friends showed up at the hospital to support us and stayed with the girls and me in the waiting room. My

Chapter 13: Where's MY Stuff?

insides felt like one of those old lava lamps where that dense blob of colored wax rises and falls with the change in heat. There was no sitting still. I just kept watching the waiting room window for someone to come and give us an update. I had prayed all I could. If God didn't know what I wanted by now, He never would.

After a long wait the doctor came in. He said, *"She's fine."*

"Did you get all of the cancer?" I asked.

"There was no cancer."

"Do you mean it hasn't spread?"

"No, there was no cancer found. She is fine. There is nothing to worry about."

Oh... that's what yes feels like.

Chapter 14

Fuhgeddaboudit

"Love... it keeps no record of wrongs."
~ 1 Corinthians 13:5

Back to Tonic

I always wondered why I wasn't angrier with the truck driver in Mexico. After all, he was the one who killed my son. He had been swept away from the accident site by a driver from a truck that came upon the scene. It is said that in Mexico there is only one of three places you will end up after an accident: the hospital, the jail, or the morgue. I guess the passing trucker was looking out for his fellow driver.

When the trucking company learned there was an eighty-thousand-dollar insurance payment available through a policy Juan bought before entering Mexico, the company sought to collect. The accident report was changed to declare Juan at fault, and an insurance claim was made. I received a subpoena. It was written in Spanish, so I gave it to a lawyer I knew in Texas who explained that they wanted me to appear at a hearing back in Mexico. He told me they were after the money and recommended I not go. I asked what would happen. He told me they would just collect the money uncontested. He said, *"Leave it be; you're not going to stop them from cashing in on the policy."*

I had good reason to be angry with the truck driver and now adding insult to injury, someone would be profiting from the deaths of Jake and the others. But my resentment went in a different direction. When it came right down to it, you could take that list I wrote about in chapter eight and scratch off all but three items because the rest of them no longer bothered me. The three that I continued to deal with were:

Chapter 14: Fuhgeddaboudit

1. I blamed Juan for the accident.
2. I blamed God for not stopping it and all that followed.
3. I blamed myself for failing to protect my son.

First I needed to deal with Juan. I never wanted to blame him, but I just couldn't escape the fact that I trusted him with my son and he failed me. There was much that I didn't know about what took place in Mexico. The accident was early in the morning and maybe Juan was pushing himself to get back to San Luis Potosi. Maybe he was tired and couldn't react to the oncoming truck. Maybe he tried to do too much in Mexico and exhaustion had taken over. I have tried to put myself in his place. It is easy to sit here now and claim I would have taken more precautions. But hindsight is 20/20. For all I knew, Juan could have taken extreme heroic efforts to safeguard Jake and the others. Why would I even entertain notions about things that may never have occurred? What I did know was that he loved those boys and sacrificed greatly to provide for them what he hoped would be a wonderful, meaningful experience. I needed to end all speculation and blame I had held against him, so I wrote these words:

"Juan, I hold no record of wrongs against you... there is nothing to forgive... and I truly mean that."

God was another matter. He wasn't exhausted. He didn't take on too much in too little time. There was nothing He didn't know. There was nothing He could not have stopped. He alone held the absolute power and ability to not only stop the accident, but to also stop all I experienced afterward. I believe my great dilemma was that as far as I could see, God did nothing. God allowed a bad thing to happen, just as He has time and time again in the lives of many, many other people throughout history. I know of no earthly action I could have taken that would have made that right with me.

Some people dedicate a great deal of time and energy to projects and memorials that have a healing effect as they insure that their loved ones will be remembered. We get a satisfaction in knowing our deceased loved ones mattered, and still do. This undoubtedly offers some comfort. But for me, there remained a lingering question. It was in those quiet moments of emptiness that I looked to God and just wondered why He didn't respond differently.

In my opinion, God made a mistake. Good boys were dead. Nothing to celebrate would ever result from it. It's true that because of what I had experienced I was able to offer help to other people at times, and I certainly came to see things that I never saw before. But in my mind, the price paid for those benefits was far too much. Honestly, I believed God had not done right by me.

I just wouldn't be able to overcome my resentment and disappointment with God until I actually accepted His authority over the very breath I breathed. I may have claimed to believe in Him and sought to submit to Him, but did I? Following God required more than just acts of service, more than obedience, more than just loving other people. It came down to the realization that all my plans, all my goals, all my ambitions, desires, and dreams were subject to His discretion. Ultimately, I really have no say or control over what may have happened then or even moments from right now. This is not and never will be my universe.

"Then the Lord spoke to Job out of the storm. He said:
"Who is this that obscures my plans
with words without knowledge?
Brace yourself like a man;
I will question you,
and you shall answer me.
"Where were you when I laid the earth's foundation?
Tell me, if you understand.
Who marked off its dimensions? Surely you know!
Who stretched a measuring line across it?
On what were its footings set,
or who laid its cornerstone—"

~ Job 38

I had to stop viewing God as a source of mammon. The only way to excuse His inaction was to acknowledge His supremacy. If I went on believing this planet I lived on was created for me, I would continue to embrace a mistaken view of God.

The Supremacy of the Son of God

"The Son is the image of the invisible God, the firstborn over all creation. For in him all things were created: things in heaven and on earth, visible and invisible, whether thrones or powers or rulers or authorities; all things have been created through and for him. He is before all things, and in him all things hold together."

~ Colossians 1:15-17

Anger aside, I did believe that God was Supreme. The Bible claimed that He loved me. I needed to end the blame I had held against Him, so I wrote these words:

"God, I hold no record of wrongs against you... there is nothing to forgive... I am the one in need of forgiveness."

Finally, there was me, the real heart of the problem. When I looked into the mirror I saw failure. I failed my son, my family, my church and my God.

A friend once told me I could find the weakness in a person quicker than anyone he had ever seen. That was the product of a bad temper and a lot of practice. I learned to control the damage that temper caused by avoiding the people who rubbed me the wrong way. That kept me from the temptation of dressing-down an opponent.

Looking back on all those years, I noticed that pattern paralleling my relationship with God. I avoided God for long periods of time because I couldn't think of a better person to blame. I knew I couldn't win an argument with God, and I was too proud to lose.

The accident was in no way my fault, but I kept second-guessing my letting Jacob go on that trip. I could have told him he was too young. He was just fourteen while the others ranged up to nineteen. This wasn't a trip planned by a Christian organization with experience in that area of Mexico. It was thrown together by Juan and a pastor down there. The boys would be traveling off the beaten path and who knew what they would run into? I felt if I'd been there to shelter him this would have never happened.

I scanned my memory, hoping to recall how Jake's participation in the mission trip came about. Could I have talked him into a trip he didn't want to take? Did he join the group because I wanted him to? Had he shown any indication of a lack of enthusiasm or desire? Did I ignore his efforts to approach me about any concerns? Did he see the on-coming truck and scream for his father's protection?

In truth, Jacob was excited about the trip. There was nothing that indicated I had forced him to go. But that thought will forever linger in the back of my mind. I had no power to protect Jacob. I only had the power to obstruct his leaving. Locking your child in a box isn't protection. Prohibiting him from going to Mexico, or Cherie from going to Africa and

Back to Tonic

Haiti, or anywhere else, wouldn't protect them. In the end, salvation is the only form of protection that matters.

Jan and I had already exposed them to the only source of protection that matters in this life; we took our children to church where they established a relationship with the Savior.

I used to say you could tell the guys who were serious about God by taking note of which ones showed up for church when their wives couldn't make it. I once was that serious. But in time, Jan turned into the spiritual rock of our family while I continued along just because I knew I was supposed to. It was part of moving on with life.

"Move on." I hate those words uttered by people on the sidelines. But I really needed to get out of the rut I'd been stuck in for so long. Wallowing in resentment only led to more resentment. Forgiving Juan, God and myself was the next step to moving on. But moving on doesn't mean forgetting or getting over our lost loved one. Instead, we should embrace that absence. Their memory, that throbbing ache and those moments of loneliness are all we have left of them. Embracing those moments instead of running from them can turn grieving death into celebrating the life we had been so fortunate to experience.

I forgave myself... and that helped me to love again.

Chapter 14: Fuhgeddaboudit

What is love?

"Love is patient, love is kind. It does not envy, it does not boast, it is not proud. It does not dishonor others, it is not self-seeking, it is not easily angered. It keeps no record of wrongs. Love does not delight in evil but rejoices with the truth. It always protects, always trusts, always hopes, always perseveres. Love never fails."

~ 1 Corinthians 13:4-8

Chapter 15

Lifting Fog

"The common eye sees only the outside of things, and judges by that, but the seeing eye pierces through and reads the heart and the soul..."[25]

~ MARK TWAIN, *Joan of Arc*

Today we live in a world where you can color your hair to make yourself look younger, paint your face to make yourself look more attractive, or have surgery to change your physical features entirely and create a *"new you."* We can make believe we are something other than we really are. But under that entire disguise, has anything really changed?

Christianity brought about a change in my actions and desires, but sometimes I wondered how much of it was cosmetic. The appearance of a changed life didn't guarantee that an entire transformation actually took place. I pursued God because I truly believed I needed Him, but undeniably I straddled the line that divided the committed from the recreational believer. I could fit into the world around me much easier as the latter.

For many people the term *"evangelical"* has become a negative expression and the term *"born again"* brings visions of judgmental attitudes. I didn't want to appear judgmental or project a sense of superiority, so I avoided discussing those terms as much as possible. An attempt to make an argument on God's behalf might have exposed that my belief was built with the stability of a house of cards.

I could declare that *"God is good,"* but after the accident I couldn't honestly point to that goodness in my life. I wasn't prepared to offer anything more than catchphrases and silly analogies to back up my claim.

Chapter 15: Lifting Fog

I thought it might be a good idea to review what motivated me to seek out God in the first place. How did I come to acknowledge Him? How did He acknowledge me? The relationship felt so real in the beginning, but had now been dormant so long I didn't know how to answer those questions.

Blind faith was all I had left to rely on and that didn't offer a very convincing argument. I could have blindly followed Buddha. The testimony for something as life-changing as finding God Almighty should have presented a convincing account of a transformation, so convincing that others would want to have what I had. There was a huge difference between striving to be a better person and pretending to be one.

As a result of the accident and all that followed I came to see myself as a weak and disjointed believer who had become satisfied with merely tagging along behind the Christian movement. My conscience prodded me to seek God, but my motivation had turned from adoration of God to primarily just wanting to be saved from hell. Christianity was my life insurance policy, not my way of life. I expected God to provide earthly comforts and heavenly rewards, believing that I had fulfilled my part of the covenant. I was plainly mistaken.

I had arrived at the crossroads and needed to decide whether or not God was still important to me. Walking away from Him would satisfy the resentment in me, but would also suggest that Jacob died for nothing. Approaching Him would require my accepting His authority over the decision to allow it all to happen. When it came down to it, I already knew which road to take.

Why Jesus

So why after all that I had been through would I continue to chase after Jesus Christ and the biblical God? The strongest reason would be because my conscience would not let me believe that God did not exist. There was an unyielding plea from within my soul to seek the truth. The worst thing that could happen to me would be to discover that God was a stranger and it was too late for me to do anything about it.

My pursuit was still in part selfish; I wanted to be saved from hell. Hell scared me. The thought of making the kind of mistake that would be eternally irreversible sent chills up my spine. Thinking back on those night terrors when my bedroom was filled with people chanting and mumbling about my fate still haunted me. My instincts led me to believe it was something more than a dream. It felt supernatural, but not necessarily evil. It was like a sampling of another dimension; enough so that there are still occasions when I uncomfortably awake in the middle of the night and fear opening my eyes.

I have been amazed at the number of people who believe in ghosts, demons, and all things supernatural, but disregard the concept of an eternal hell. It seemed many people see heaven as a place they just naturally end up when life is over, as if it were some kind of default setting. Realistically, if I believed in a place called heaven, it would have been foolish of me to think my performance here on earth warranted a blissful reward.

I've often wondered if people who claim there is no afterlife remain that confident on their death beds. I once watched a television documentary about people nearing death. One segment was about a man who had throughout his life claimed to not believe in God or the afterlife. He was begging the doctors to do whatever they could to keep him alive. He flailed about in his hospital bed like a sky diver whose parachute had failed to open and was now plummeting toward the ground at an ever-increasing rate of speed. Earthly life was all this man knew and he seemed terrified of what might be coming next. He had put off contemplating an afterlife and was now desperately begging for more time to think about it. Apparently, something within him was shrieking out a warning like a mother trying to stop her child who was about to run into the path of a speeding automobile. I think we call that conscience. No matter how bold our claims, our conscience seems to have the final word.

Agnostics hold the view that man does not currently have the necessary facts and/or reasons to provide a rational argument to justify the belief that God either does or does not exist. How long will they wait to decide? To not sincerely consider what comes after this life seems such a huge gamble, yet people continue to defer decisions on eternity until a more urgent moment forces them to choose a side.

My pursuit of Jesus Christ is driven not only by a fear of hell, but also by a love for God that necessitates a relationship. It's difficult to explain how that originated. It becomes comprehendible to some extent when I equate it to my love for my own father.

I wasn't born loving my dad; I was subjected to his love. I loved him because he loved me first. I loved his love for me well before I loved him as a person. He was the source of my wellbeing and without him I would not have survived. He held me, housed me, fed me, clothed me, disciplined me and unconditionally loved me. He sacrificed for me in ways that demonstrated his commitment to me. I didn't grow to love him as a person until I came to know him as a man, which differs from knowing him as a father.

As a child I called out for my dad when I was afraid. As an adult, I—and most everyone else—call out to God in moments of desperation, regardless of what we claim to believe. There is no such thing as an agnostic conscience; it recognizes Him who formed it and needs no further proof of His existence. The conscience has been acquainted with God since its conception.

"Before I formed you in the womb I knew you..."
~Jeremiah 1:5

Chapter 15: Lifting Fog

I can understand where my dad's love for me came from because that is how I loved Jacob. I also understand how Dad's love came with no prerequisite on my loving him in return. Once when Jake was a little boy he got angry with me because I took away a toy he was misusing. Jake kicked me in the shin and threw punches at me as he screamed in anger. I reached out and grabbed him. Pulling him close to me, I held him, hugged him, kissed him and let him know how much I loved him. But he didn't get the toy back that day.

I opt for Jesus Christ because I realize perfection is unattainable. If heaven is the home of flawlessness I will never earn a heavenly reward. I'd be only fooling myself to think I could achieve a faultless life by doing good deeds and loving people. I have already tried *"do-it-yourself religion"* and it blew apart in the storm. I required a belief that would accept an offender like me; a failure in need of a Savior. Every other religion promotes the thought that you can earn heaven on your own merits. Christianity is the only one that calls it like it is.

"For all have sinned and fall short of the glory of God."
~ Romans 3:23

I believe most people are pretty naive when it comes to acknowledging the Creator of heaven and earth. I am taken aback by those whose greatest moment of commitment to God is attending church on Christmas and Easter. I wonder how many of them could locate a Bible in their homes, much less turn to the verse in the Book of John that they are often so critical of:

"I tell you the truth; no one can see the kingdom of God unless he is born again."

~ John 3:3

They act as if that comes out of some crazy cult instead of the mouth of Jesus Christ. They don't grasp the concept of their need of forgiveness. Maybe that's because they have never been humbled enough to ask for it.

Some people get hostile when they hear Christians talk about atonement. They just don't believe that forgiveness comes with the asking. One guy told me he couldn't accept the notion of a person living an awful life and then being forgiven without penalty by simply saying, *"Sorry."* He was *"tired of hearing about that damn born again [stuff]."*

I had a simple response for him. There are two things he didn't understand about God. First, God is not an idiot; He can tell the difference between words and repentance. Second, the Bible is clear on this: He is a God of justice. He does not allow sin to go unpunished. Sin owes a debt and someone is going to pay that debt. He could pay that penalty himself if he really wanted to, or accept God's offer to pay it for him.

I challenged him to at least take a moment to consider what the next life might be like because eternity lasts a *"long damn time,"* and it's worth thinking about prior to arriving there.

What good is it to endure this life only to lose the next? How sad would it be to know you bypassed spending eternity with the Creator of all things because of your own pride or apathy?

> *"Justice is not always done in the world; we see that every day. But on the Last Day it will be done for all to see. And no one will be able to complain saying, 'This isn't fair.'"*[26]
>
> ~ *Donald A. Carson, PH.D.*

Knowing what's fair is directly related to knowing God. Knowing God is the product of knowing His word. Knowing His word is the compass to straight paths.

> *"Your word is a lamp to my feet and a light to my path."*
>
> ~ *Psalm 119:105*

When I hunted, I would go out pre-season and pick a spot to build my stand. That spot usually ended up being a pretty good walk from where I parked my truck. On opening day I would head out to that spot early in the morning. Shooting hours began a half hour before sunrise. That meant I needed to get there well before that. I would set out in the dark. I knew the way, but I was walking through some rough terrain. It would be easy to trip and fall or get turned around in the dark and end up in the wrong section of the woods. A flashlight would be handy, but I didn't want to announce to every deer in the county that I was in the woods. Instead, I'd bring one of those tiny pen lights and shine it right at my feet so I could see where I was stepping and avoid tripping.

Too bad I wasn't as wise about precautions in everyday life as I was in the woods. I spent most of my time tripping my way through life because I failed to use the *"lamp"* God provided for me to clearly light my way.

When I kept repeating the verse from Proverbs in my truck on the way home that awful day in July what I was really asking was for God to trust me with this life He had given me. I wanted all of His heart to follow what my heart desired. I wanted God to acknowledge me. I wanted Him to take my path. I expected Him to hear my voice... on my timetable... on my terms.

> *"...You cannot fast as you do today*
> *and expect your voice to be heard on high.*
> *Is this the kind of fast I have chosen,*
> *only a day for a man to humble himself?*
> *Is it only for bowing one's head like a reed*
> *and for lying on sackcloth and ashes?*
> *Is that what you call a fast,*
> *a day acceptable to the Lord?*
> *Is not this the kind of fasting I have chosen:*
> *to loose the chains of injustice*
> *and untie the cords of the yoke,*

to set the oppressed free
and break every yoke?
Is it not to share your food with the hungry
and to provide the poor wanderer with shelter—
when you see the naked, to clothe him,
and not to turn away from your own flesh and blood?
Then your light will break forth like the dawn,
and your healing will quickly appear;
then your righteousness will go before you,
and the glory of the Lord will be your rear guard.
Then you will call, and the Lord will answer;
you will cry for help, and he will say: Here am I.
If you do away with the yoke of oppression,
with the pointing finger and malicious talk,
and if you spend yourselves in behalf of the hungry
and satisfy the needs of the oppressed,
then your light will rise in the darkness,
and your night will become like the noonday.
~ Isaiah 58:4-10

Apparently God Himself had laid down some conditions that govern whether or not my voice would be heard on high. My selfish and haphazard attempts at acknowledging His authority over all things did more to block my access to Him than to open any doors. It only makes sense that God would expect things to be done his way. It only makes sense that the Creator of heaven and earth would be afforded the privilege of setting the rules—all of them. I was expected to abide by His wishes, not make what I deemed rational adjustments so His will would agree with mine.

I also had to take into consideration that His own personal suffering was part of His will. God purposely came to earth to suffer and die so that unworthy people could one day escape the sorrow of earth and enter into a perfect eternity with Him. With that in mind, how could I complain about His will for my life?

Honestly, I don't believe God caused the accident. I don't think it was part of some *"plan"* of His. I think it was the tragic result of a series of free-will decisions that came together where heaven met earth on that rural highway outside San Luis De La Pas early on that July morning. I think God showed up there that morning, and like a person sorting through the scattered pieces of a spilled jigsaw puzzle, He collected those pieces and reassembled them in such a way that tragedy would be turned into hope. I believe He saw an opportunity to open my eyes. And He has.

I am by no means a model of Christianity. I struggle daily. I'm not going to pretend I have been transformed into a Billy Graham or Mother Teresa, but I have an understanding of my position in Christ Jesus. I do recognize what it is like to have questions and doubts. As a result of wrestling with those doubts, I am a stronger person today. I'm not afraid to ask for some clarity. And most importantly, I get along with the words of the Bible. I don't fight them anymore. I am able to allow the light of the *"lamp"* to illuminate my path. I don't necessarily need to know what lies over the hill; I only need to be reminded to Whom the hill belongs.

Chapter 15: Lifting Fog

My hope remains in Jesus Christ because there is nothing else that can provide hope to a sinner like me. I cannot earn my way to heaven; He is, without doubt, my only chance.

Above all, I believe He loves me.

Chapter 16

Taking Up the Baton

"The most beautiful people we have known are those who have known defeat, known suffering, known struggle, known loss, and have found their way out of the depths. These persons have an appreciation, a sensitivity, and an understanding of life that fills them with compassion, gentleness, and a deep loving concern. Beautiful people do not just happen."[27]

~ *Elisabeth Kübler-Ross*

Back to Tonic

There was yet one thing left undone. I needed to finish what Jacob started. I needed to pick up the baton and carry it through to completion; if for no one else, for me. I could not rest until I drew to a close Jacob's journey. There should have been a joyous return. There should have been a celebration. There should have been stories to share and memories to savor. If I couldn't see Mexico through Jake's eyes, I could see Haiti through my own.

Haiti isn't Mexico, but it's similar in terrain, the litter, the poor, and, oh yes, the traffic. The same reckless driving habits that led to Jake's death were routine on the roadways of Haiti. Experiencing that again was somewhat nerve-racking.

I have been told that Haiti has long accepted voodoo and the country has been cursed because of a pact made with Satan.

"In 1791, Dutty Boukman, a slave and Voodoo priest led a ceremony where he prophesied that three slaves would lead a revolt to free the other slaves of Saint-Domingue. An animal was sacrificed and a vow was taken. Boukman encouraged those listening to take revenge against the French and cast aside the image of the God of the oppressors. Blood from that animal and some say from humans as well, was given in a drink to the attendees to seal their fates in loyalty to the cause of liberation of Sainte-Domingue. Within a week, 1800 plantations had been destroyed and 1000 slaveholders

Chapter 16: Taking Up the Baton

killed. This ceremony came to be characterized as
the "pact with the devil" that began the Haitian
revolution... the French left in 1803... Haiti has been
impoverished ever since."[28]

~ *From Wikipedia, the free encyclopedia*

I have also been told that Haiti is a beautiful country, but that section of the island must have escaped me. I found it to be a hot, desolate tract of rocky landscape. Even the remote areas of the hilly terrain were decorated with litter. It looked as if Haiti served as the world's trash can.

Who would want this Haiti? Apparently God does. He's sending missionaries there constantly. My flight from Atlanta to Port-au-Prince was probably seventy-five percent missionaries heading off in all different directions of Haiti.

In 2010, a devastating earthquake displaced 1.5 million people. Three years later, nearly a half-million people were still homeless, many living in Cité Soleil, the worst slum in the Western Hemisphere.

Relief groups have been engaged in rebuilding efforts there, and I wanted to witness Haiti's rising back from disaster. Much like my own climb from the rubble left behind by the accident, if what was being rebuilt there in Haiti was not founded in God, it would at some point crumble and fall again. Resetting God as the cornerstone of Haiti's foundation instead of Voodoo would bring about great hope for its future; imagine what could rise out of it.

I needed this. If Jake could look down and see what his death had done to me he might have needed it as well. I wanted to again experience life in a third world country, only this time without the heavy burden of mourning loss and retrieving bodies. It would feel so good to share in Jake's excitement instead of lamenting the memory of his ill-fated Mexican trip. It would be healing for me to finally bring to close the journey Jake began. I needed a new and positive experience that might reinforce the principle of sending missionaries out into such places.

I really didn't want to travel across the continent just to hug orphaned kids and pass out goods. I was looking for a greater purpose in my mortal being. I'm no minister or inspiring speaker and saw nothing of value within me to offer. If God can use all things for his glory, how would He purposefully use an ordinary person like me in a place like Haiti? Could I submit to whatever tasks waited there?

I had an empty place in my soul waiting for an assignment to fulfill. I have served in many different roles within the church body over the years and have to honestly admit that every one of them has felt somewhat foreign to me. I don't believe I have ever made a lasting contribution to *"God's Plan"* because I cannot identify my having added anything of worth. Could

Chapter 16: Taking Up the Baton

Haiti provide me with some direction for the remainder of my life?

When I stepped off that airplane into the oven-like heat of the chaotic airline terminal in Port-au-Prince, I stepped out trusting that God not only would provide me with safety, but He would provide me with purpose.

Yes, you read that correctly. That was me saying I was trusting God with my safety.

I had joined a group of four others at the airport in Chicago. We represented the World Compassion Network's first visit to The Mission of Hope. This was my team, and I think God may have handpicked them just to make me feel at ease. Our flight was uneventful, but locating our bags and leaving the airport in Port-au-Prince was quite an experience in itself. The extremely hot and crowded terminal provided little information or order. Guessing our way through the un-boarding process, we finally gathered our bags and headed out the door to what seemed like a hundred-yard dash through a gauntlet of Haitian men grabbing at us and wanting to carry our luggage or offer directions in French Creole, a language I did not understand. Their purpose was to earn tip money, which in itself was not that unusual, except that if nine men put a hand on your bag, all nine of them believed they were entitled to a tip.

I convinced myself I was going to trust God on this trip and that is what I set my heart to do, but my mind wasn't completely sold on the idea. Standing in the sweltering sun alongside a chain link fence at the edge of the parking lot, we waited on the mission bus for an hour or so. Hot and uncomfortable, I began to wonder if this was all a mistake. I'm a list maker; I like to know what is happening and when it's happening. I don't do well waiting in the scorching sun, surrounded by yelling Haitians and with no idea what's going on.

Everything seemed so disordered. Haitians are loud talkers; I couldn't tell if they were angry or if it was just normal conversation. U.N. troops patrolled the city streets and from what I was seeing, that seemed like a good idea. Vans with armed men hanging out the doors sped past with horns blaring. Brightly painted buses and pickup trucks known as *"tap tap cabs"* packed with people resembling sardines in a can raced about as if there were no traffic laws. The whole area seemed incredibly frenzied. I'm told that traffic signals are there just for decoration. It was all quite a sight to behold.

Gradually, some other missionaries wandered our way, and we realized we were all heading to the same place. Men from the mission finally arrived and began loading our bags into a truck as we boarded the mission's bus.

Once on the road, the wonderment of a third-world country caught my attention. Haiti had the appearance of a war-torn region.

Chapter 16: Taking Up the Baton

I could almost picture Jacob sitting next to me sharing the excitement. I recalled the twinkle he would get in his eye when he was encountering a new adventure. He would have been sitting on the edge of the seat, staring out the window, absorbing the distinctive differences in the way of life found there. I started getting really excited about what lay ahead for me.

As we pulled up to the mission campus we saw armed guards manning the gate and patrolling the perimeter. Jake would have loved this! I could picture him filled with enthusiasm, spinning his head back to look at me with wide eyes and finger pointed to make sure I didn't miss seeing what he was seeing. We were told the mission was guarded because in times of disaster, starving people stop at nothing to gain access to food.

After getting settled in, I walked to the mess hall for my first Haitian meal, hotdog buns filled with cheese, lettuce and tomatoes. Somehow I was expecting the Haitian cuisine to be somewhat different. That was followed by a meeting to discuss the weekly agenda and then some fellowship to get to know each other.

Lightning streaked across the night sky, leaving remnants of glowing reddish-orange shades of color beyond the distant mountains. I climbed up to the roof deck of the bunk house to watch. This storm reminded me of the thunderstorm that accompanied me on the plane ride home from Mexico. However, this storm wasn't taking me with it; instead, it was leaving me behind. It felt like I was watching the passenger train that just dropped me off at the station pull away and disappear down the tracks. It felt like I had just received the baton.

After a very sultry and sleepless night in a bunk room shared with six other men and several geckos, we all got up at 5:00am. Breakfast was waiting at the mess hall—more Haitian cuisine—bananas and bread. Then we were taken on a walking tour of the main campus where we saw the school, orphanage, medical center, prosthetic lab, warehouse and some of the other areas in which we might be working in the week ahead.

The tour ended at the open air church where things were about to get started. A comfortable breeze blew through the audience. The church service went on for about two and a half hours. Although the sermon was in French Creole, of which I recognized about five words, I knew what was happening because I followed along in my Bible the verses listed in French Creole on the overhead screen. It wasn't all that hard to figure out.

How fitting was it that this particular sermon, on this particular day, was about trusting your faith? Did God know I was in the audience or what? The dialogue was beautifully rhythmic. I knew what was being preached in spite of the fact that I didn't speak the language. God was speaking directly to me; not in audible words, but in a clear heartfelt understanding of the message. I hadn't felt Him at that level since I'd first called out to Him that cold January night in my backyard nearly forty years earlier.

That was my favorite moment in Haiti. I was part of worship and adoration in its purest form. It left me with a Spirit-filled excitement that kept me awake that night as I basked in a personal moment with God. Another *Close Encounter of the Third Kind*!

When people have little or nothing, nothing gets in the way of their worshiping God. There was an excitement that reenergized me. I may have not been empty when I walked in the door but I left fuller than I could have imagined.

After visiting two additional campus sites I was eager to be given some responsibility. Busloads of missionaries were to be sent out into the villages each day to paint cinder block houses, provide meals and help with Bible school classes. I was hoping for something more exciting, but fully expected to be part of that outreach. After overhearing a conversation between several full-time staff workers, I learned that some projects were on hold due to broken equipment. I have spent forty years working on the railroad. I know a lot about repairing the un-repairable. I offered to take a look at the equipment and was immediately pressed into service.

My first project was repairing a windmill and pump that supplied water to the agricultural training site. With two other men and very limited tools, I repaired and replaced the damaged components. Making use of a team of willing Haitians, a length of rope and our truck, we hoisted the structure back to an upright position. Those blades beginning to revolve in the wind brought a smile to my face and a real sense of accomplishment.

I was the square peg meant for that square hole. Feeling right at home, I welcomed the responsibility and went on to repair anything I could get my hands on. I installed overhead lighting in a classroom, repaired an oven used to mold thermoplastic prosthetic limbs, and got a number of all-terrain vehicles up and running again. I also worked for several days with a group of men erecting a huge metal roof three stories above a bunk house.

The experience offered a clear picture of how the church works like a body with many parts, each performing different functions that all come together to produce one great purpose. Every part within the body is necessary. As a result of my abilities, I saw myself as a crucial part of the unit.

Marienatha

The devastation in Port-au-Prince from the earthquake will be felt for years by people whose limbs were traumatically crushed by collapsing buildings. It's hard enough to negotiate that terrain with two good feet. It would be nearly impossible to get around in a wheelchair.

I had been hiking back and forth on the rocky campus road of the Mission of Hope for several days. Everything was either uphill or downhill and I developed a blister on my foot as a result of the constant climbing. I tried to ignore the discomfort and work around the nuisance.

I was called down to the prosthetic lab to take a look at the molding oven that wasn't working. Favoring my foot as I limped down the road, I spotted Marienatha. She was hobbling ahead of me with her mother. This sixteen-year-old was also heading to the prosthetic lab where she was being fitted for a left foot and a right leg. She made her way down the rock-strewn road by wobbling her weight back and forth from the sandal strapped to the shin of her right leg stump to the partial foot of her bowed left leg. Her mother held her by the forearm because Marienatha had no hands. This was her life. My blister no longer bothered me.

It was hard to fathom how that young girl survived like this. There were no taxi cabs dropping her off. Her mother didn't own a car. This was how Marienatha moved about day after day through that brutal terrain. All I could think at that moment was, *"Thank God, that isn't me or one of my children."*

Marienatha took her first steps in an upright position with her new prosthetics the week I was there. She was assisted by

Sam, a friend I met at the campus. That was a healing time for both of those beautiful people. Sam had lost her left arm in a motorcycle accident. She came to the mission in Haiti hoping to find some answers as well. She sought to discover God's direction for her newly-altered life. Sam made me smile.

Haiti is a good example of a people *"moving on,"* recovering from great devastation. Not just the earthquake; Haiti is rebounding from its history of Voodoo worship and great poverty.

The simplicity of life there took me back to my childhood. As a kid we played in our backyard. We didn't have lawns and swing sets, we had dirt piles and wagons. We loved it! Laying in my bunk in Haiti, I remembered what it was like in our house on hot sweltering summer nights. I never felt underprivileged because I had to sleep in a hot room. I didn't know there were any other options. Hot nights were just what we expected from summer.

We didn't have patios and lawn furniture. When we had a family picnic, we carried the kitchen table and chairs outside and we thought we had it made because we actually had chairs outside to sit on. We were happy, and even more importantly, we were content. When I contrasted that time so long ago with the present time and all the comforts I now had, I realized I was at an advantage back then. Relating to God was easier because, like in Haiti, there wasn't much to get in the way of it. I was satisfied. I didn't feel cheated, I felt at home. It made me wish I could go back to the way it used to be, back to the beginning.

I loved Haiti. It brought me back to my boyhood. It brought me back to adventure. I'm sure that is what Jake loved about Mexico. Haiti allowed me to connect with Jacob again. Being there reminded me of the time I touched the low-hanging tree branches that lined the walkway in San Luis Potosi and envisioned the boys walking down that path and touching them in the same way.

I could picture Jacob doing what I was doing in Haiti, and loving every minute of it. What stories would he have come home with? What would have been his greatest delight? How excited would he have been to pass on his experiences to the rest of the family? How much would it have impacted his future life?

Isaac

I received my own special delight my last day there; Hurricane Isaac. I love storms, and I had never witnessed a hurricane. Oddly, out there in the middle of nowhere, I was able to text Jan on my cell phone. We had no access to news other than cell phones. Jan was concerned because the hurricane was coming right at us and she asked if it was possible for me to get out before it hit. My reply to her was simple, *"Are you kidding? This is a gift. I've always wanted to experience a hurricane."*

Back to Tonic

The goats that forage outside the campus fence seemed to know something was coming. They stood motionless with arched backs as if bracing for the oncoming storm. The clouds were decorated with bands of blue, orange and yellow. As night approached, I pulled my bunk to the open door of my room and watched what I could see through the dark.

The storm came with an unrelenting shrill wind that sounded like a jet engine. A tree snapped just outside the door. I was in awe of the power of the storm as it hurtled through the campus like an endless high-speed freight train roaring down the track. It was exhilarating!

I felt like I was sharing that moment with Jacob and became that fourteen-year-old boy one last time. Oh, how I missed that! It demonstrated how flashes of harmony could be found in the most unexpected places; like a violent storm, or maybe even a terrible accident.

Making our way home the day after the storm proved to be a long, exhausting process hindered by delays. I stood in one spot in the suffocating airport with a crowd of people swarming up against me for nearly three hours.

I may have lost my happy face about an hour into the delay, but I really was okay with it because of what I was taking home with me. I had a new clarity of purpose and, most importantly, I was bringing Jacob home; not as a box of ashes, but as a whole and accomplished life. His mission was now complete.

Chapter 17

Back to Tonic

"Faith is the strength by which a shattered world shall emerge into the light."[29]

~ *Helen Keller*

Back to Tonic

I play a little guitar. I like The Blues because I understand it. As long as I know what key is being played, I can get up and join the band because I know where the music is going. The 12-bar blues progression has a distinctive chord structure and duration. The beginning of the progression is called "tonic." The cadence moves from the tonic to dominant, to subdominant, and back to tonic again. The dominant function has the role of creating instability that requires the tonic for resolution.

This repeats itself throughout the song, returning to tonic each time after an ending segment called the *"turnaround."* I can feel the turnaround coming. Similar to the force of gravity, it draws me back to the start of the progression. Without returning to the beginning of the progression the song has no resolution. It just wanders on without direction or purpose in search of a return to tonic.

I've experienced that same pattern within the spiritual periods of my life. They have moved from strong to weak at different times, but I've always sensed the urge to return to a healthy relationship with God. This time the transition proved to be strangely complex. I wasn't returning to the same old concept of God I'd held before.

This attempt was met with some reservation and I wasn't confident I wanted to restart the relationship. The notion that I would never find a suitable answer for Jake's death this side

Chapter 17: Back to Tonic

of heaven was hard to swallow. Nevertheless, I viewed Jesus Christ as being an absolute necessity in my life.

Regaining tempo, I did my best to not just reconnect with God, but to do it under His terms. That often resembled Marienatha's slow progression up the road to the prosthetic lab: painful, beleaguered, and grueling. The struggle proved to be worth the effort for both her and me as in the end we were able to stand tall again.

Twenty years after the accident, my pastor Randy was moved to sobbing when, while conducting a funeral service, he came across Jake's burial chamber in the wall of the mausoleum. Randy never knew Jacob. There before him, displayed on the wall was the reality of another promising life lost, and there was just no good earthly explanation for it.

I'm sure Randy had seen his fill of the suffering and emptiness that result from human loss. I've wondered if pastors ever run out of consoling words or if they ever just simply reach a breaking point. Curious as to what brought on the tears; I asked Randy why he cried.

He explained that he had conducted more burials or graveside services at that cemetery than any other in his 11 years serving at Deer Creek, and he was back in the same room for another interment. When the service concluded he looked around and found the name of a person he'd buried just one month earlier. He decided to take a minute and read all the names in the front of the Mausoleum.

Randy was in a very reflective and introspective mood that day. He was feeling real empathy for the family to which he had just ministered and was imagining all the families and friends represented by those whose remains were all around him in the walls.

Just then, as he read the names on the front wall, Jacob's caught him by surprise. He'd seen Jake's crypt years earlier but had forgotten it was there. For the first time he actually took notice of all the boys' names. He immediately imagined what that season was like for my family. He wondered how it felt for all the families that shared the same loss, and for their community of believers.

Randy said as his tears began it was like life flashing before his eyes. He quickly retraced everything he knew, read or heard about those days. He remembered the written account of what I went through in Mexico. His stomach churned as he imagined the hurt and pain.

He recalled the words of the scriptures he had just shared in the earlier service and thought, are they true? If they are true, then those young men in Jacob's group are not dead; they are only sleeping. Their souls are alive, but their bodies are at rest. They are waiting for the day of the resurrection where the dead in Christ will rise first. In this life there is hope because of the resurrection of our Lord and Savior Jesus Christ.

"Where is the proof?" he asked himself. *"How do I know there is hope and power over the grave? How do I know that my redeemer lives? How do I know that the faith will be made sight?"*

Randy answered his questions with this: *"Because I have seen the hope, the power and the faith in my friends Gene, Jan, Janene and Cherie. I respect the journey their lives have experienced; everything from the days of Jacob's fatal accident in Mexico all the way up to today. Faith is not defined by tragedy; Faith is defined by how people like my friends have overcome tragedy with endurance, continuing the journey of faith."*

I was humbled by Randy's response and how he saw such faith in me, the very man who was surely the worst example of it. One thing I did know: the greatness of God is only visible in me because of the measure of faith He implanted and would not allow me to throw out. No matter how much I wanted to, I could not deny God.

"When you and I hurt deeply, what we really need is not an explanation from God but a revelation of God. We need to see how great God is; we need to recover our lost

*perspective on life. Things get out of proportion when we
are suffering, and it takes a vision of something bigger
than ourselves to get life's dimensions adjusted again."*[30]

~*Wiersbe*

Good Grief

Homeless Earl has to eat... I have to have God. Both of our
survivals depend on it. Much like Earl, humility is what
enabled me to beg. My pleas went out to God Almighty and I
tossed aside the Build-a-Bear model of God I'd been working
on for so long.

I came away from all this with two main truths. The first
truth was admitting the brokenhearted reality of my never
being able to share this life with Jacob again. We'd never
have another time to hunt and fish together. That chapter of
life is gone. I wouldn't watch him mature to be the man I
envisioned him being. He wouldn't marry and have children
of his own. There would never be a next chapter... but there
will be a final chapter.

That final chapter is dependent on the second truth; either
I believe in God or I don't. I couldn't simply choose not to
believe. Something inside wouldn't allow me to deny my
Creator. I deliberated day and night to resolve the issue of a
God who did not act. I threw stones at God and I never got
the reaction I wanted. My soul screamed for an explanation
that never came. I felt like I was the target of a relentless

pursuit. Finally, at the brink of mental collapse, I looked back and asked, *"Who is that guy?"*

I could no longer support the idea of a God who does not have complete authority over all He created. The idea of a limited God is really kind of asinine. Who would want a God Almost-Almighty? Who would want a God without authority over His creation—all of it—even Jacob's life? I will no longer be duped by the great human flaw which promotes the idea that God is accountable to me.

In the end, my grief proved to be beneficial. I learned from it. I came to know myself in ways I never could have otherwise. I am more confident of salvation now than I ever was before. Today I know the God who is not restricted by limitations imposed on Him by me. I don't need to lead, I merely need to follow. And that has lifted the weight from my shoulders.

A Note to the Doubter

I heard someone say, *"If that's the way God is, I don't want anything to do with Him."* That got me thinking. What would be the other option? Could a person really prefer to spend their eternity somewhere other than heaven? That decision would be eternally irreversible. It's not like merely choosing the wrong color to paint the bedroom walls.

I can completely understand the inner fervor that boils against God when we find Him to be in opposition to our hearts' desires. I understand what it's like to feel ostracized. That experience felt so awful I was convinced of one thing: I didn't want to maintain that feeling for all eternity. The question of eternal life begs for a well-thought-through decision.

The Bible is filled with the accounts of great men of faith who went through periods in their lives when they questioned God's sovereignty. From Jonah's fleeing Nineveh to Elijah wanting to never have been born, men have been challenged in their walk with God.

Questioning one's faith is not a sign of weakness. It reveals a soul-searching quest for God. Some of our biggest pillars of faith such as David and Jacob wrestled with God. Jesus himself cried on the cross: "*My God, my God, why have you forsaken me?*" These examples clearly suggest that questioning God is an acceptable practice.

But also consider Job. In God's response to Job, He offered no explanations. Instead, God pointed out that the situation was far too immense for Job to ever comprehend. Job needed to find rest in the sovereignty of God.

Although your struggle may last an earthly lifetime, don't throw eternity away over a misunderstanding. Keep seeking, keep praying, keep clinging. Don't give up. Don't ever quit in your pursuit, because God will not turn you away.

Chapter 17: Back to Tonic

Don't let your pursuit be for answers: Let it be for God.

A Note to the Consoler

There are a few other benefits gained as a result of my journey. If asked my opinion on how to console a grieving person my first response would be, help them cry. Remember, there are no magic words. What may make sense to you most likely won't to them. Little or nothing will.

If at all possible, remember the date of their loss and send them a short note letting them know you continue to remember. Don't be afraid to reminisce. If they begin to talk about their loss, drop everything you're doing and open your ears. Keep them open as long as they are willing to let it out.

Finally, don't think you are an authority on the Bible simply because you've read it. I would recommend that instead of bombarding a grieving person with verses, bombard them with prayer and ask the Great Healer to address their broken lives.

A Note to the Griever

If you are suffering from grief, know that denying your pain isn't healthy. Believing it is your duty to be an example for others puts off your own healing. When offered condolences, accept them knowing that the words can't always express what their hearts feel. Never feel compelled to respond with clichés like, "They're not suffering anymore," unless you really mean it. That reply may be true, but while they may no longer be suffering, don't dismiss the reality that you might be. Don't lessen YOUR loss. Consolers show up for your benefit. Take advantage of their expressions of sorrow even if they're not good at it.

Grieve your lost loved one. Don't let anyone take that right away from you. Grieve them as long as you need to. Never let yourself bury their memory away. There is no altering what has happened. Life changes and the sun will rise again tomorrow, but that is no reason to abandon the memory of the person you knew and loved before. Try to transform your thoughts from focusing on the death to celebrating the life and relationship you had enjoyed so much.

I have come to accept the fact that Jacob is no longer here with me physically, but he continues to be a part of my life because there is no taking away the person he was. His footprints are embedded deeply in my everyday life. Jacob is now a very warmhearted memory, and I embrace that memory. I still have moments of sadness and emotional pain, but I embrace them as well because that is as close as I can get to him these days. Hurt as it may, I love that presence.

I have also come to accept that I was lukewarm in my faith. It was so much easier relating to a god who was of my own formation. That generic god was designed for my happiness, and in a sense, I grieved the loss of that comfortable relationship. It didn't require much from my end.

Chapter 17: Back to Tonic

That god failed me. It took me a while to recognize my mistaken conviction. That part of grieving lasted longer and was much harder to deal with.

Having stopped my obsession over what could have been, I convinced myself to look at my life for what it was. Could I identify anything beneficial to come away with? Today, I find myself saying this out loud more and more: "In my desperation I truly met God. My grief was good." I have received my "revelation of God." I allowed Him to take His rightful place as the Authority over my existence. By doing that I recovered my perspective on life.

God, being who He is, can use all things for good, but I'm not looking for that one great reason that would make Jake's death seem worthwhile. I will take nothing in trade for my much-loved Jacob. However, if God wants to use this whole ordeal for His glory, count me in. I carry no more expectations for this life, but I have high expectations for the next. Through God's grace alone I have all that really matters in the end—atonement for my sin as a result of the death and resurrection of Jesus Christ.

Yes, we do need to move on. The world around us continues to move forward and we have to keep up with it. Keep in mind that there is going to be remembering and there is going to be grieving; nonetheless, the funeral must stop. So we get back up on our feet, but we don't get up empty. We take with us the strength we've acquired through our struggle and a clearer picture of our God Almighty.

There is one truth that seems beyond my reach: Complete rest from my worries can only come if I commit every single part of my life to God. I haven't done that yet. I don't know that anyone can honestly claim that.

I have decided to take my art teacher's advice and learn to see before I draw. It took the accident to show me how. I was never one to let myself cry. Today I weep, but not as a person who has lost hope, because I know that in dying Jacob has arrived at his great reward in the Land of the Living. And I know that when I see him next, it will be an eternal reunion in a place where there will be no tears; a place of matchless blessings and beauty beyond our imagination.

The scar of Jake's death will vanish from sight. The question of God's divine providence over events in my life will matter no more. Peace will be at hand. It will be then that I will absolutely find myself to be "back to tonic."

Epilogue

Back to Tonic

Back to Tonic started twenty years ago as nothing more than the private journal of a desperate man who had been drowning in his own grief, and as a result, suffocating spiritually. Back then, I would have been reluctant to let another soul read what I wrote, let alone publish it. I wrote because it was a way to release some of what was bottled-up inside. It was the outlet that kept me from exploding.

Sitting at the computer one day, I opened a new Word document and titled it "*Thoughts.*" In the months to come, I let my heart bleed in the form of text typed on the page: all of my emotions, all of my questions, all of the details of my experiences. It was the only place where I allowed myself to truly express my innermost struggles. I never imagined sharing those pages with the world.

Some friends suggested I write a book about my experiences. Having been a poor student of English, I used to joke that I could hardly spell book, let alone write one. Nevertheless, as a result of encouragement from my wife and daughters, and an appeal from several others who found my struggles familiar, I decided to explore that possibility.

Beyond dealing with the loss of Jacob and all that followed, Jake's unfinished mission trip had always bothered me. I felt I owed it to him and to myself to bring to a close what he had hoped to realize. While I had repaired my relationship with God and written the majority of the book years before

Epilogue

my trip to Haiti, it was upon returning from that trip that I considered the journey finally at an end.

People handle things differently; this is my account of life after tragedy. This book is meant to not only help people like myself, but also to make others aware that we exist. My hope is that this story will provide a way for those who find themselves in the valley of the shadow of heartache, emptiness, and isolation, to come to a place where they can know that <u>God really is good.</u>

Back to Tonic

Endnotes

1. Joseph Campbell
2. Adam LaRoche
3. Henry L. Gilmour
4. Winston Churchill
5. C.S. Lewis
6. Leo Buscaglia
7. Pat Spalla
8. Chinese Proverb
9. Joanne Zapchenk
10. Joanne Zapchenk
11. Arleen Duffy
12. Arleen Duffy
13. Harriet Beecher Stowe
14. Goldie Hawn
15. Maya Angelou
16. Jake's Journal
17. Areli
18. Charles Spurgeon
19. Church growth expert Win Arn
20. S. I. Hayakawa
21. Benjamin Franklin
22. Found scratched into the wall of a Nazi Concentration Camp.
23. Dr. Barbara L. Fredrickson
24. George Weigel Christian Number-Crunching - Feb 9, 2011
25. Mark Twain, Joan of Arc
26. Donald A. Carson PH.D
27. Elisabeth Kübler-Ross
28. Wikipedia
29. Helen Keller
30. Wiersbe

CPSIA information can be obtained at www.ICGtesting.com
Printed in the USA
LVOW11s1843150614

389925LV00002B/2/P